A Guide to
Twentieth Century
Portraits

Paul Moorhouse

National Portrait Gallery, London
in association with the National Trust

Published in Great Britain by
National Portrait Gallery Publications
National Portrait Gallery
St Martin's Place
London WC2H 0HE

In association with the
National Trust
Heelis, Kemble Drive
Swindon, Wiltshire SN2 2NA
www.nationaltrust.org.uk

For a complete catalogue of current
publications please write to the National
Portrait Gallery at the address above, or visit
our website at www.npg.org.uk/publications

ISBN 978 1 85514 460 6

A catalogue record for this book is
available from the British Library.

10 9 8 7 6 5 4 3 2 1

Managing Editor: Christopher Tinker
Editor: Andrew Roff
Design: Thomas Manss & Company
Production Manager: Ruth Müller-Wirth
Printed and bound in Hong Kong

Picture credits

Front cover
Detail from **Paul McCartney (*Mike's Brother*)**
by Sam Walsh, 1964, see p.46.
Back cover
Paul McCartney (*Mike's Brother*)
by Sam Walsh, 1964, see p.46.

Inside front cover
Anna Zinkheisen self-portrait, *c.*1944, see p.33.
Inside back cover
T.S. Eliot by Patrick Heron, 1949, see p.36.

Contents

Introduction

The twentieth century was an era of radical, sweeping developments, often occurring in quick succession, which transformed almost every aspect of civilised existence and human endeavour. An individual born in 1900 occupied a new world, one that saw man take to the air through powered flight and, within a lifetime, set foot on the moon. These two feats alone – the conquest of gravity and the exploration of the heavens – define the astonishing scope of achievement. By the end of the millennium, the boundaries of experience had been re-drawn, decisively and irreversibly.

But scientific progress and technological innovation were only facets, albeit vital ones, of a century impatient to build upon yet break with the past. The invention of the internal-combustion engine enabled the creation of the aeroplane and led to the design of the space rocket. Such advances had their roots in the important engineering accomplishments of the Industrial Revolution. However, during the twentieth century, the machine age entered a new phase, the effects of which spread to every corner of life. Responsive to the acceleration of activity and communication, and the widening perspectives offered by science, the arts sought new means of expression to convey the sense and significance of the modern. Painting, sculpture, literature, drama and music all shed conventional ideas and practices in their exploration of new imagery, forms and emotional messages.

Political, public and private life were similarly swept along by powerful social currents, which, while positive and liberating, were neither predictable nor controllable. During the early years of the century, the role of women commenced a prolonged and profound departure from its historic antecedents. For some, such as writer and gardener Vita Sackville-West and novelist Radclyffe Hall, this involved challenging conventional attitudes to sexuality. At the same time, two devastating world wars were a stark reminder that the modern world had its darker side, marked by an enhanced and unprecedented capacity for destruction. Inevitably, this altered human landscape found its

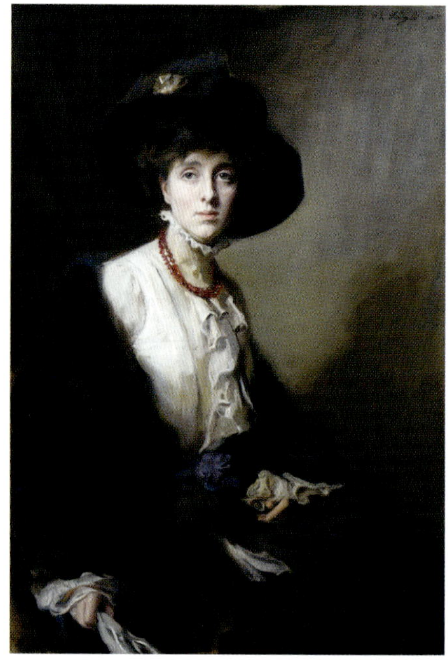

Vita Sackville-West (1892–1962)
Philip de László (1869–1937)
Oil on canvas, 1910
1200 x 830mm
Sissinghurst Castle, Kent

reflection in alternative patterns of behaviour, morality, beliefs
and attitudes. At the beginning of the twenty-first century,
the legacy of the preceding age remains potent. Confidence and
anxiety are enmeshed with a continued appetite for development,
accompanied by deepening concerns about the future of the planet.

Modernism and tradition

The trajectory and character of recent events were not determined
by accident or by natural forces. The tide that coursed through
the developed world in the twentieth century was set in motion
by individuals. Modern life was brought into existence by human
beings acting collectively, as well as by certain remarkable figures
who, single-handedly, made a different or original mark on the
matrix of everyday events and, in so doing, changed the destiny
of their fellow beings. Such singular figures are protagonists in
an immediate way: they are the principal characters in a wider
drama, agents for change and, frequently, the champions of
particular causes. They also represent a wide range of human
action and achievement. There are those who have affected
the fabric of the world in tangible ways: scientists, engineers,
architects and designers; at another extreme there are those
whose contribution is more abstract but no less powerful:
writers, thinkers, critics and politicians. Between these
poles, the wide middle ground is a meeting place where action
and ideas come together. This includes artists, entrepreneurs,
explorers and leaders in sport, to name but a few areas of
endeavour. Some individuals crossed these boundaries, the writer
and soldier T.E. Lawrence ('Lawrence of Arabia') achieving an
almost mythological status. All have coloured the map of the
modern world in different ways.

The Twentieth-Century Collection at the National Portrait
Gallery reveals much about the appearance and configuration of
that map. It is commonplace to characterise the twentieth century
as the age of modernism. The dizzying pace and profusion
of innovations, styles and ideas – from wireless telegraphy to
the invention of the Internet – have, rightly, given rise to the
impression of relentless advance. Modernism is connected
with an infatuation with the new. In the arts, the Modern
Movement applied a reforming zeal to all forms of expression,
from architecture and painting to music and literature.
Modernism expressed a belief in the validity of the unfamiliar,
a stance that at times has bewildered and alienated its detractors.

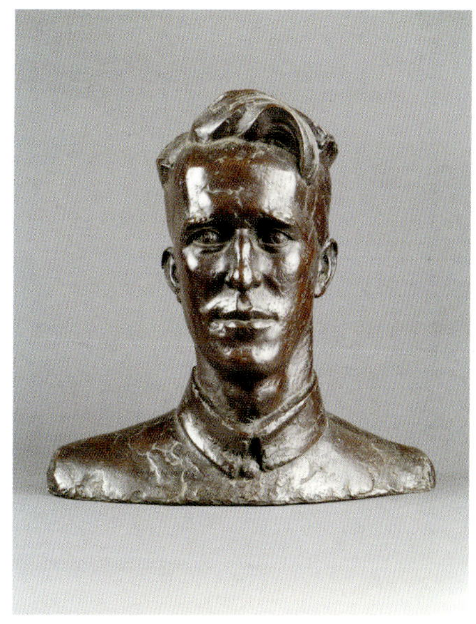

T.E. Lawrence (1888–1935)
Eric Kennington (1888–1960)
Bronze bust, 1926
413mm high
Clouds Hill, Dorset

Undoubtedly, the idealisation of progress stands at the centre
of the century of change. But, as the portraits in this book
show, that progressive ethos was not embraced by all artists.
Alongside masterpieces of modernism such as Patrick Heron's
highly abstracted painting of T.S. Eliot (p.36), there are numerous
portraits of an altogether different cast. For example, Lucian Freud's
portrait of the financier and patron of the arts Lord Rothschild
(p.56) was painted forty years after the Heron portrait.
However, being rooted in direct observation from life, the
later work is arguably much more indebted to tradition.
How is this apparent paradox to be understood?

As part of its wider collecting remit, the Gallery's twentieth–
century portraits depict individuals connected with recent British
history and culture. They evoke a cultural scene linked to a particular
country at a specific time. But in Britain the relation of modernism
to tradition was complex. While modernism was international
in scope, it took different forms according to its host country.
In France, for example, where the Modern Movement largely
originated, it had a visible, mainstream presence for most of the
period under discussion. This contrasted with the situation across
the English Channel. In common with the rest of Europe and North
America, Britain resonated with the impact of modern life;
the nation was no less in thrall to cars, trains, wireless, cinema
and changing fashions. Following the Second World War, and
increasingly after the 1960s, television, mass production, popular
culture and the latest technological advances were as evident in
Britain as elsewhere. However, as this selection of twentieth-
century portraits shows, in relation to the Modern Movement,
the situation was ambivalent.

Secure in its island position, between the wars Britain remained
cut off from and, as a result, largely cautious about those modernist
artistic innovations that it associated with the Continent.
For example, Ambrose McEvoy's 1919 portrait of Sir John Alcock
(p.19), the celebrated aviator, is a compelling image but essentially
traditional in manner. Its conservatism is apparent when taking into
account that, by that time, Picasso's invention and early exploration
of Cubism was complete, its impact on the European avant-garde
profound. But, until 1945, for most members of the British public,
and for more traditionally minded artists, Picasso was simply a
rumour that evoked suspicion. That situation was not helped when
in 1949 Sir Alfred Munnings, President of the Royal Academy,

Wyndham Lewis (1882–1957)
Self-portrait
Pen, ink and wash on paper, 1932
304 x 228mm
NPG 4528

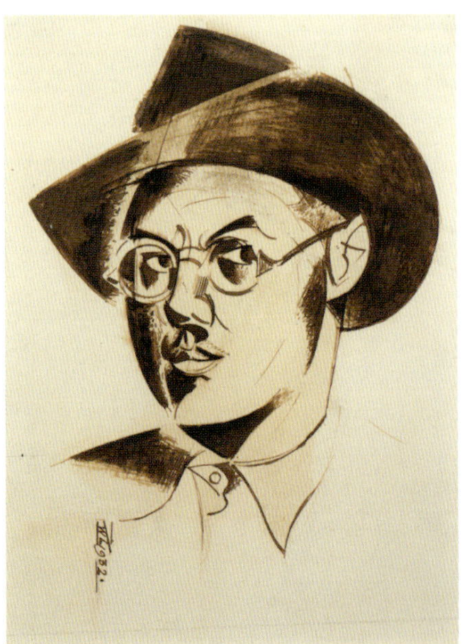

denounced 'so-called Modern Art' in a notorious RA Annual Dinner
speech that was broadcast to the nation.

Munnings's antipathy to modern art was by no means
ubiquitous. But there is no doubt that he voiced a hostility to, and
an ignorance of, more advanced forms of visual expression that
were shared by many in Britain until the 1950s. There had been
earlier opportunities to view the works of European masters
such as Cézanne, Matisse and Gauguin in important exhibitions
held in London in the first decade of the century. Following
that, in 1910–11 and late 1912, two landmark Post-Impressionist
exhibitions were organised by the critic Roger Fry. Among a
receptive minority, these events were profoundly influential.
Such revelations of avant-garde art abroad spawned pockets of
modernist innovation in Britain during the period preceding
the First World War. The most notable manifestations were
the Camden Town Group; painters such as Duncan Grant
and Vanessa Bell, who were associated with Bloomsbury;
and Wyndham Lewis and the Vorticists. In 1914, an exhibition,
Twentieth Century Art: A Review of Modern Movements, was held at
the Whitechapel Gallery. This chiefly comprised British artists
working in more progressive styles. However, such growth was
short-lived. The First World War drained the incipient Modern
Movement in Britain of energy, prompting a return to order and
a continuing reliance on familiar, conventional artistic modes.
During the inter-war years, there continued to be exceptions,
most conspicuously in the hands of Ben Nicholson, Barbara
Hepworth, Henry Moore, Wyndham Lewis, John Piper and John
Banting. In the main, however, the impetus of early modernism in
Britain was lost and remained the preserve of a distinguished few.

The diversity of modern portraiture

In essence, the problem was abstraction. Picasso and Matisse had
led painting to an involvement with shape and colour for their
own sake, liberated from literal depiction. At this, the forces of
tradition in Britain balked. Artists trained at the Royal Academy
and the Slade School of Fine Art were reminded constantly of
the example of the historic past, the need for fidelity to natural
appearances, and the value of conventional skills in drawing,
composition and perspective. Undeterred by those experimental
forces at work in Europe, in Britain tradition and innovation
co-existed in the visual arts. A surprising consequence is that,

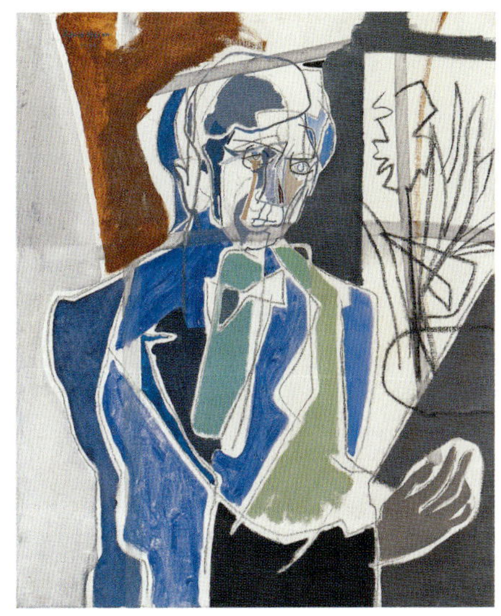

Sir Herbert Read (1893–1968)
Patrick Heron (1920–99)
Oil on canvas, 1950
762 x 635mm
NPG 4654

nourished by these inimical influences, portraiture not only
continued but also flourished.

While its conventional raison d'être remained that of
depicting the appearance of the sitter, during the inter-war years
the language of portraiture advanced on a broad front. At one
extreme, Glyn Warren Philpot's compelling portrait of Sir Oswald
Mosley (p.20) and Augustus John's image of Dylan Thomas,
c.1937–8, retained a commitment to naturalistic description.
At the other, Ben Nicholson's double portrait of himself and
Barbara Hepworth (p.27) inhabited an imaginative realm
involving abstracted shapes and lines. Between these poles,
a rich terrain is apparent. Masterly portraits by Mark Gertler,
Paule Vézelay, Walter Richard Sickert and John Banting configure
the landscape of individual achievement. In their work,
a complex balance is struck between fidelity to their sitter's
appearance and a celebration of painting for its own sake.

Having renounced modernism, after the Second World
War the forces of officialdom progressively embraced and
supported the avant-garde. In 1945, the Victoria and Albert
Museum hosted an exhibition of paintings by Picasso and
Matisse. Beginning with the establishment of the Arts Council
in 1946, the mission to increase public access to fine art
focused on the purchase of modern British art. The opening
of the Institute of Contemporary Arts in 1947 was a further
spur to progressive visual forces. Its co-founder, the writer
and critic Sir Herbert Read, influenced the growing profile of
more avant-garde tendencies. In 1952, his selection of post-
war sculptors for the British Pavilion at the Venice Biennale
brought international attention and conferred a title on an
emerging generation: 'the geometry of fear'. Modern art
also became increasingly visible at other London galleries,
including the Tate Gallery, the Whitechapel and a range of
dealers' spaces.

This expanding acceptance of modern art is reflected in
the National Portrait Gallery's holdings of post-war portraits,
in which a growing diversity is apparent. Kenneth Green's
portrait of Benjamin Britten and Peter Pears (p.30), Anthony
Devas's portrait of Laurie Lee (p.32) and Anna Zinkeisen's self-
portrait (p.33), all of which were completed between 1943 and
1944, are evidence of a continuing adherence to tradition.
During the 1960s, the outlook began to widen. In 1968, for
example, the Gallery's dynamic new director, Roy Strong,

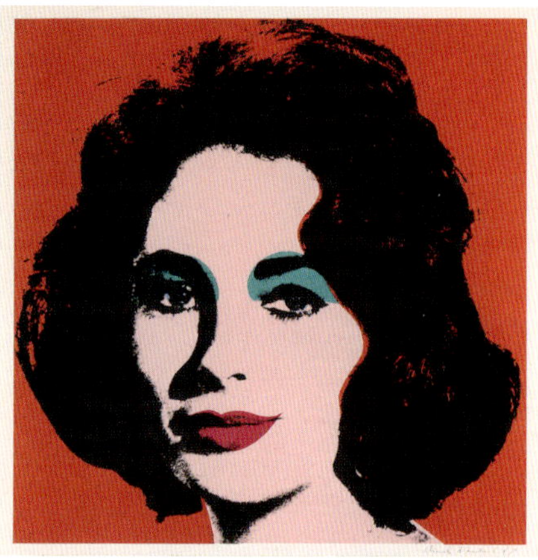

Dame Elizabeth Taylor (1932–2011)
Andy Warhol (1928–87)
Offset lithograph, 1967
559 x 559mm
NPG 6051

wrote to Henry Moore, thanking him for his gift of Patrick Heron's portrait of Herbert Read. Strong also intimated an interest in acquiring a portrait of Moore. He observed: 'As you know I am trying to liven up this faded gallery and am cautiously wandering into the present.' Augmented subsequently, in the Gallery's representation of the 1960s a broader view is evident. Portraits by Howard Hodgkin, Larry Rivers and Andy Warhol demonstrate the challenge to literal observation posed during this period, while in the medium of photography David Bailey and Eve Arnold manifested a new, distinctive vitality.

The stylistic diversity that characterises the Gallery's representation of post-war portraits had, by the end of the century, found a new rationale. Having secured acceptance and a place within twentieth-century portraiture, modernism can now be seen as an integral part of a wider pattern in which tradition and experiment coexisted. With the advent of post-modernism, a growing freedom to range across different styles meant that photography and other media increasingly enriched the repertoire, extending the range of image-making. As his 1996–7 portrait of the film-maker Derek Jarman shows, artists such as Richard Hamilton explored the relation of painting, photography and computer technology. At the threshold of the new millennium, all these approaches had been embraced by portraiture. They provide alternative means of evoking a human presence, signifying achievement and expressing experience, in the modern world.

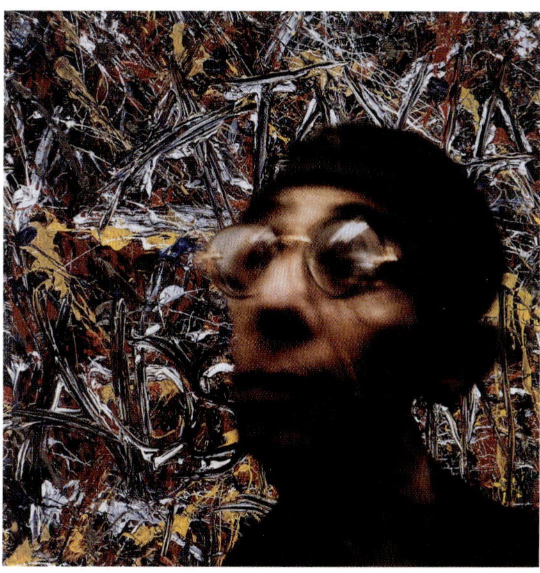

Derek Jarman (1942–94)
Richard Hamilton (1922–2011)
Pigment transfer, 1996–7
390 x 390mm
NPG 6680

The early twentieth century

The years between the death of Queen Victoria in 1901 and the outbreak of the First World War in 1914 witnessed a complex evolution in British society. Queen Victoria's passing brought to a close her sixty-four-year reign and seemed to signal the end of an era. However, as Sir Luke Fildes's portrait of her successor, Edward VII, suggests, regal dignity and splendour were a visible connection with Britain's stately, imperial past. In society as a whole, formal codes of dress and behaviour continued to define a hierarchical and divisive structure linked to tradition.

Even so, a succession of new developments increasingly challenged entrenched ideas and, as a result, widened the horizon. In 1903 the first powered aircraft was flown in North Carolina. That same year the first transatlantic radio transmission, a message from President Theodore Roosevelt to King Edward VII, was sent from the United States to London, where motor taxis now appeared on the streets, following the earlier introduction of motorcycles. In 1909, Sir Winston Churchill, then a member of Herbert Asquith's cabinet, caught the mood of change: 'We have arrived at a new time. Let us realise it. And with that new time strange methods, huge forces, large combinations – a Titanic world – have sprung up around us.' But ambition and progress came at a price. In 1912,

Captain Robert Falcon Scott's mission to reach the South Pole ended in disaster. Later that year, 1,513 lives were lost when RMS *Titanic*, the world's largest and most luxurious passenger liner, hit an iceberg and sank on her maiden voyage.

In the visual arts, exhibitions held in London in 1906 and 1908 devoted to the work of Cézanne, Matisse and Gauguin made a connection with the European avant-garde. The formation of the Camden Town Group in 1911 marked the absorption of modernist ideas. Also, following the two Post-Impressionist exhibitions held in 1910–11 and 1912, Vanessa Bell's informal portraits of Roger Fry and her sister Virginia Woolf demonstrated a growing engagement with unconventional ideas and abstracted painting styles. This developing rapport with the European avant-garde was, however, cut short when in 1914 Britain became embroiled in a long and debilitating war.

King Edward VII
Sir Luke Fildes (1843–1927)
Oil on canvas, 1912, replica of his
1902 portrait
2756 x 1803mm
NPG 1691

Edward VII (1841–1910) was the eldest
son of Queen Victoria and Prince Albert.
As Prince of Wales he was excluded
by his mother from any involvement
in affairs of state. As a result, until
his accession in 1901, his time was
devoted to socialising and pleasure-
seeking. However, he proved an able
monarch, conscious of his position and
responsibilities. He oversaw an era of
prosperity, the age associated with his
name coming to symbolise a golden era
before the catastrophe of the First World
War. His close attention to correct,
formal dress and the trappings of status
was legendary. Fildes's state portrait of
1902, of which this is a replica, was the
first to be exhibited at the Royal Academy,
following the dearth during Queen
Victoria's long widowhood. It shows the
King wearing a field marshal's uniform,
a form of military dress that had not
changed since the 1880s.

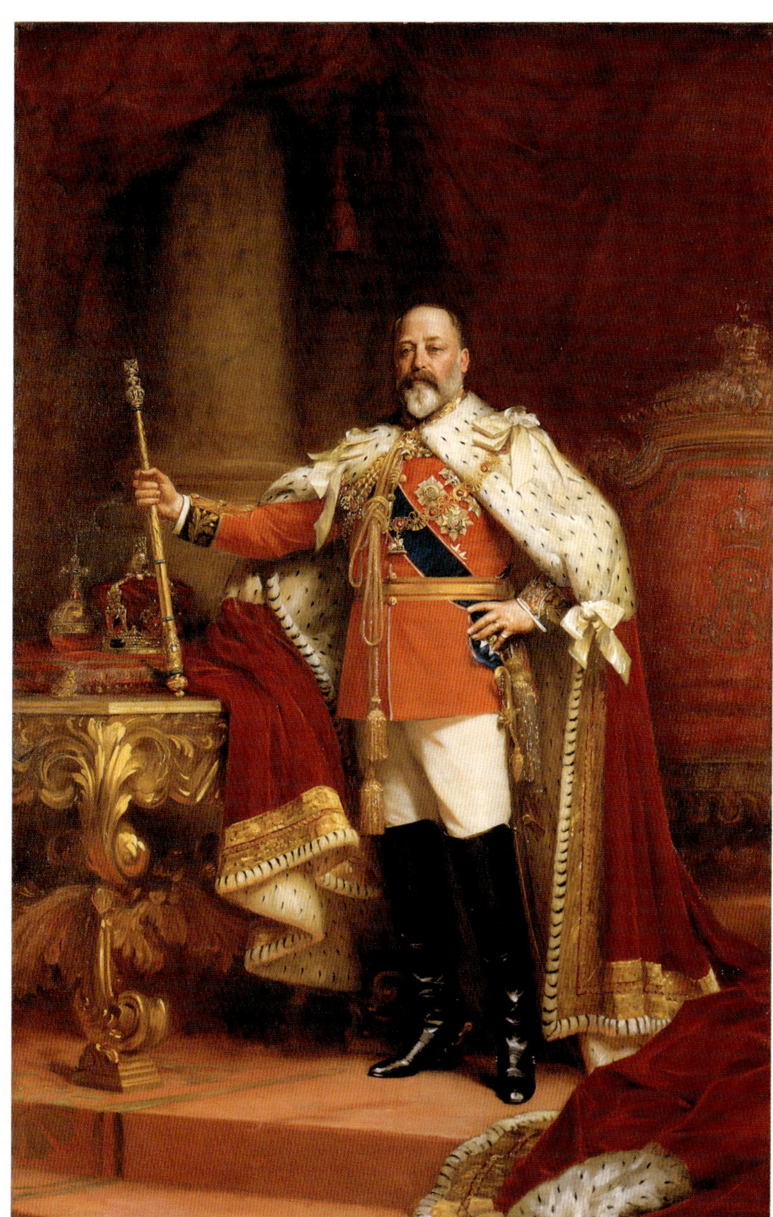

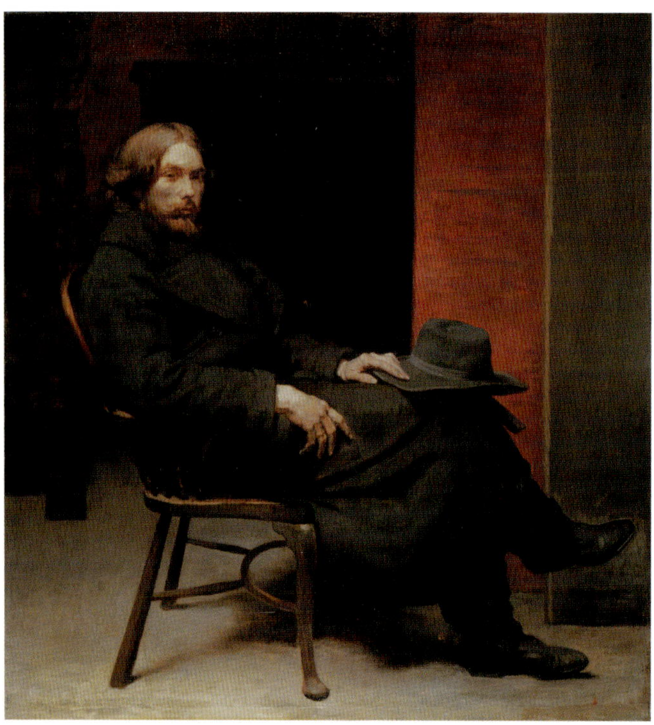

Augustus John
Sir William Orpen (1878–1931)
Oil on canvas, exhibited 1900
991 x 940mm
NPG 4252

Augustus John (1878–1961) was a leading figure of the Edwardian avant-garde. Legend has it that, following a head injury sustained while swimming, his personality and artistic powers were transformed. He became a brilliant, rebellious and flamboyant student (1894–8) at the Slade School of Fine Art, his drawings celebrated for their fluent vigour. He later studied with his sister Gwen in Paris. Following his return to London, in 1903 John was elected to the New English Art Club (NEAC). Orpen, who entered the Slade in 1897 and became a close companion, made his debut at the NEAC with this portrait. However, the sitter disliked it, claiming it showed the 'legend', rather than his truer, dreamy self. John was a prolific portraitist, whose sitters include the artists Jacob Epstein, William Nicholson and Wyndham Lewis and the writers Thomas Hardy and George Bernard Shaw. His later work was, however, adversely affected by a bohemian lifestyle.

Gwen John
Self-portrait
Oil on canvas, c.1900
610 x 378mm
NPG 4439

One of the foremost women artists of the twentieth century, Gwen John (1876–1939) painted this self-portrait at the beginning of her career, aged about 24. John trained at the Slade School of Fine Art from 1895 to 1898, where she won a prize for figure composition. Subsequently she spent several months in Paris at the recently opened Académie Carmen, studying under Whistler, who paid tribute to her 'fine sense of tone'. She returned to London in 1899 and began to exhibit her work there. This portrait appears to date from that time. Its air of confident assurance contrasts with her description of herself then as 'a waif'. After four years she returned to Paris where she settled permanently. She modelled for Rodin, with whom she had a long affair, and exhibited regularly in the Paris Salons. This portrait was owned by her brother the painter Augustus John until his death in 1961.

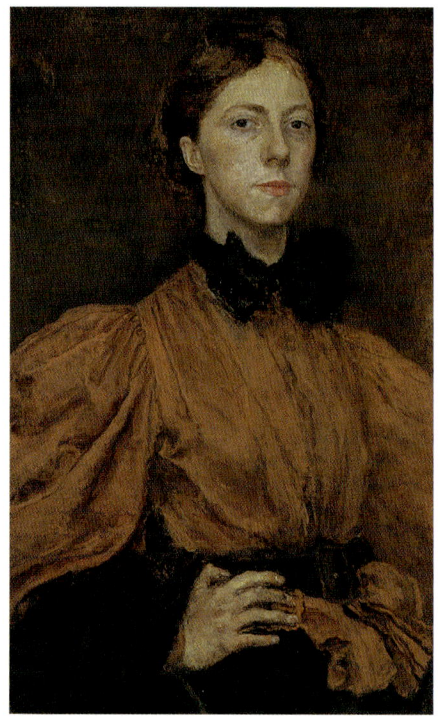

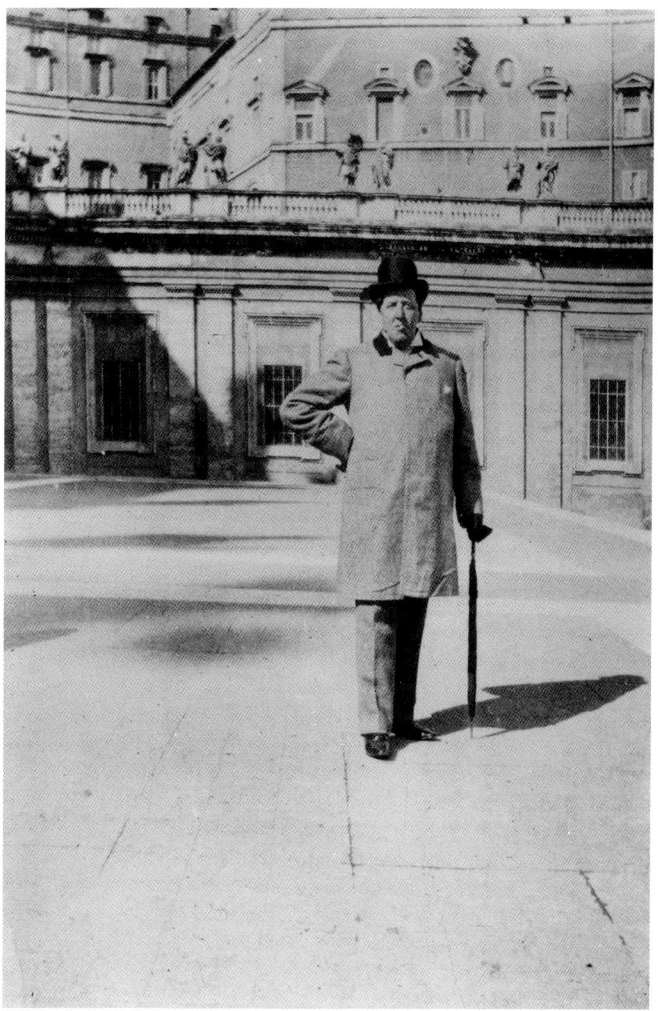

Oscar Wilde
Unknown photographer
Snapshot photograph,
spring 1900
82 x 60mm
NPG P317

Irish writer and wit, Oscar Wilde (1854–1900) was renowned as an aesthete, his unconventional and eccentric behaviour and dress attracting both notoriety and celebrity. The Aesthetic movement, which cultivated 'art for art's sake', was exemplified by Wilde's art and life. During the 1880s he established himself as a brilliant conversationalist, his paradoxical and epigrammatic observations often forming part of his highly successful comedies staged in the early 1890s. In 1895, his association with Lord Alfred Douglas led to an accusation of homosexuality by Lord Alfred's father, the Marquess of Queensbury. Wilde lost the ensuing court action and was imprisoned, his career and reputation in tatters. This photograph depicts Wilde during a visit to Italy, following his release from prison. Having scandalised the society of his day, Wilde's homosexuality is now an accepted part of his reputation as a leading cultural figure.

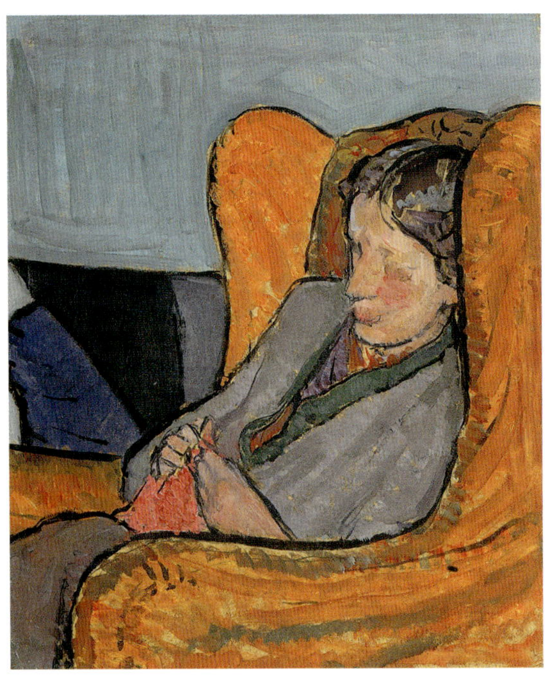

Virginia Woolf
Vanessa Bell (1879–1961)
Oil on board, 1912
400 x 340mm
NPG 5933

As early as 1908 the great modernist writer Virginia Woolf (1882–1941) declared her intention to 'reform the novel'. In the books that followed her first, *The Voyage Out* (1915), she developed her concern with internal monologue. Moving away from conventional narrative and characterisation, this technique evoked a stream of mental impressions. As central figures within the Bloomsbury Group, both she and her sister Vanessa Bell were committed to exploring new ideas in relation to literature and the visual arts. This intimate portrait, one of four painted by Vanessa between late 1911 and mid-1912, was completed shortly before Virginia's marriage to the publisher and political writer Leonard Woolf. At this time she was working on her first novel. In its use of abstracted form and heightened colour it reveals Vanessa's response to the Post-Impressionist exhibition held at the Grafton Galleries in the winter of 1910–11. The National Trust's historic house, Knole, in Kent provided the inspiration for Virginia's novel *Orlando* (1928), and the Woolf's country retreat Monk's House, Sussex is also a National Trust property.

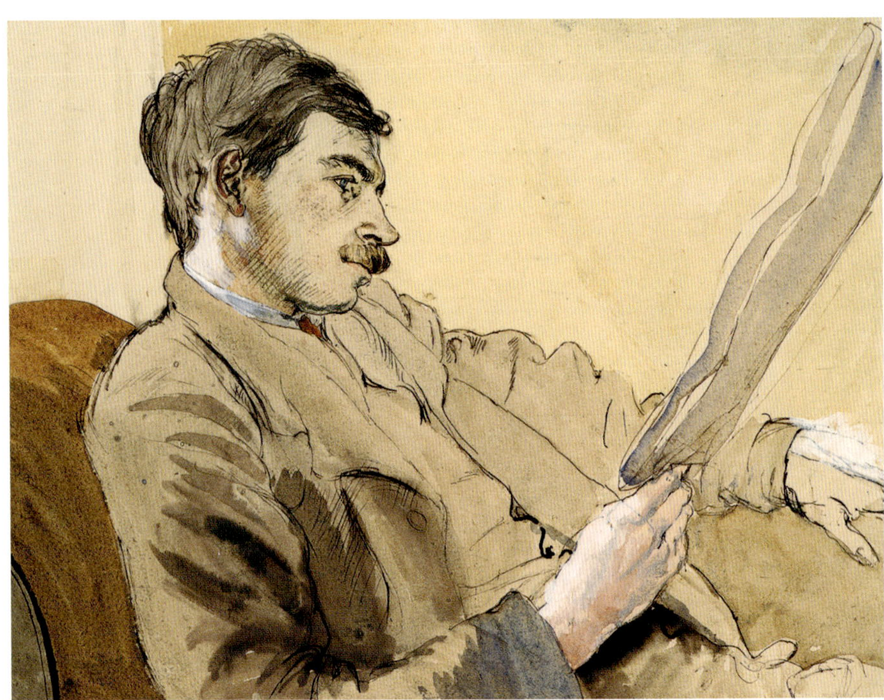

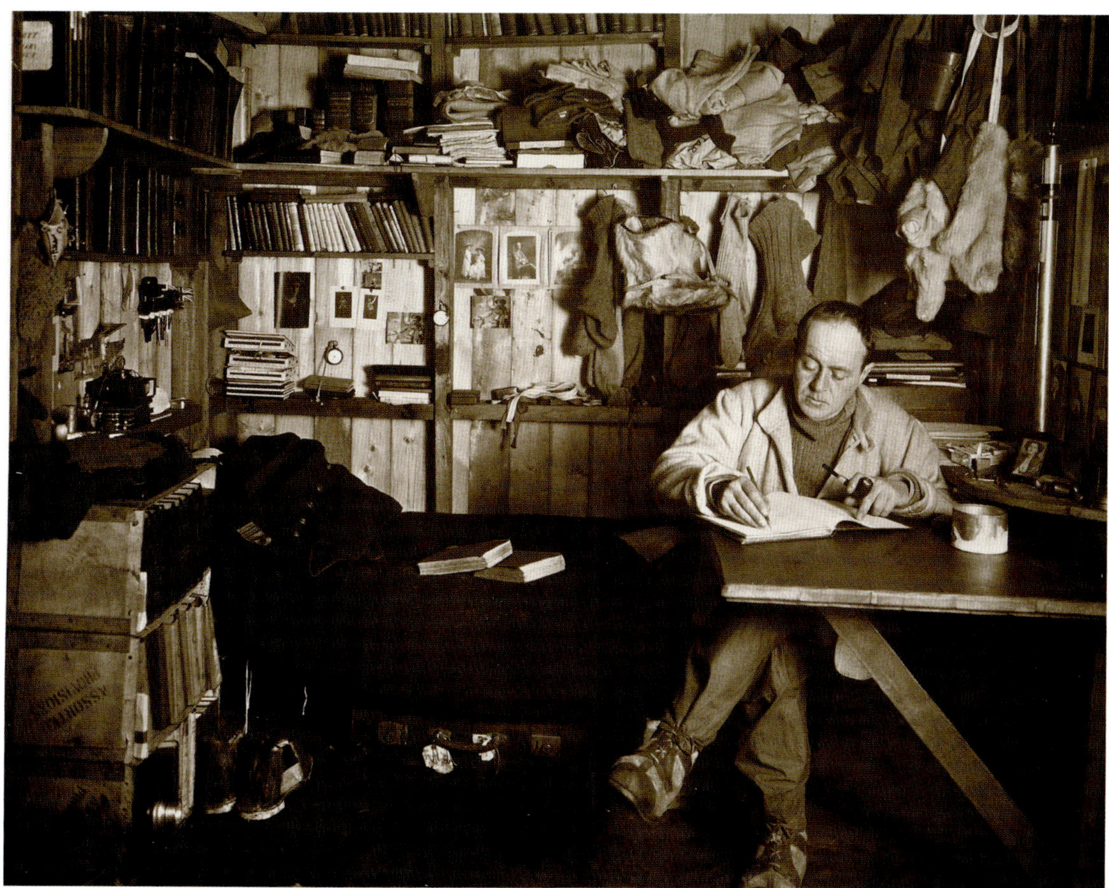

John Maynard Keynes
Gwendolen ('Gwen') Raverat (née Darwin) (1885–1957)
Pen and ink watercolour, c.1908
279 x 368mm
NPG 4553

John Maynard Keynes (1883–1946) was the most
important economist of the twentieth century.
As an undergraduate (1902–5) at King's College,
Cambridge, Keynes met Lytton Strachey and Leonard
Woolf. That association led to his membership of the
Bloomsbury Group of artists, writers and intellectuals
that included Vanessa Bell, Virginia Woolf and Roger
Fry. The Group's avant-garde ideas extended to ethics
and personal relationships, areas in which it departed
from convention. This informal watercolour drawing
depicts Keynes around the time he was a lecturer at
King's College, Cambridge, and before he became
editor of the *Economic Journal*. He held that post from
1912 to 1945 and through it exercised great influence.
The artist, a granddaughter of Charles Darwin, was a
friend of Vanessa Bell and became Keynes's sister-in-law.

Captain Robert Falcon Scott
Herbert George Ponting (1870–1935)
Carbon print, 7 October 1911
356 x 457mm
NPG P23

One of the twentieth century's earliest heroes, sailor
and explorer Captain Robert Falcon Scott (1868–1912)
led two British Antarctic expeditions. The first (1901–4)
reached further south than any previous attempt.
The second, which started in 1910, reached the
Antarctic on 22 January 1911. This photograph by
Herbert Ponting, the expedition's official photographer
and cinematographer, shows Scott working on his
journal at the base camp at Cape Evans. In addition to
an array of paraphernalia – including socks, binoculars,
family photographs and a naval overcoat – there is even
a complete set of the *Dictionary of National Biography*.
Scott set out three weeks after this photograph was
taken. He reached the South Pole on 17 or 18 January
1912, only to find Roald Amundsen's Norwegian
flag awaiting his arrival. Overwhelmed by appalling
conditions during the return trek, Scott and his three
companions all perished.

The Great War and its aftermath

Europe was decimated by the First World War, with appalling losses on all sides. It is estimated that Britain's war dead numbered around one million. Among these, the poet and artist Isaac Rosenberg was killed on the Western Front in April 1918. His self-portrait, completed only three years earlier, stands as a poignant reminder of a life cut down in its prime. In 1915 the anarchic Modernist movement Dada took root in Zurich as a response to the war. In contrast, one of the immediate effects of the conflict in Britain was to bring to an end the progressive Vorticist movement and to provoke a widespread return to order. Even so, the period that followed was marked – socially, politically and artistically – by continuing change and also by uncertainty and instability.

The role of women, in particular, remained volatile. In 1914, a suffragette attacked Velásquez's painting, the *Rokeby Venus*, in the National Gallery. Charles Buchel's 1918 portrait of Radclyffe Hall is sexually ambiguous, anticipating the scandal that ensued when Hall's novel, *The Well of Loneliness*, was banned for its portrayal of lesbian love. In 1922, the BBC began regular radio broadcasts, thus marking the onset of mass communication that would be a dominant engine for social change. In 1924, the first British Labour government was formed under Ramsay MacDonald.

Oswald Mosley joined Labour that year, but he left subsequently, forming the British Union of Fascists in 1932. Glyn Philpot's portrait of Mosley, although penetrating, is conventional in manner. It contrasts with Paule Vézelay's self-portrait, painted around the same time, which demonstrates a leaning towards abstraction. But Vézelay's affinity with more advanced modes of visual representation was out of step with the conservative British art world, and she later forged closer links with Parisian avant-garde. In France and Germany the Modern Movement took shape in the form of Surrealism and the Bauhaus. In Britain, portraiture continued, with paintings by Maurice Lambert, Mark Gertler and Ernest Procter striking a balance between tradition and innovation.

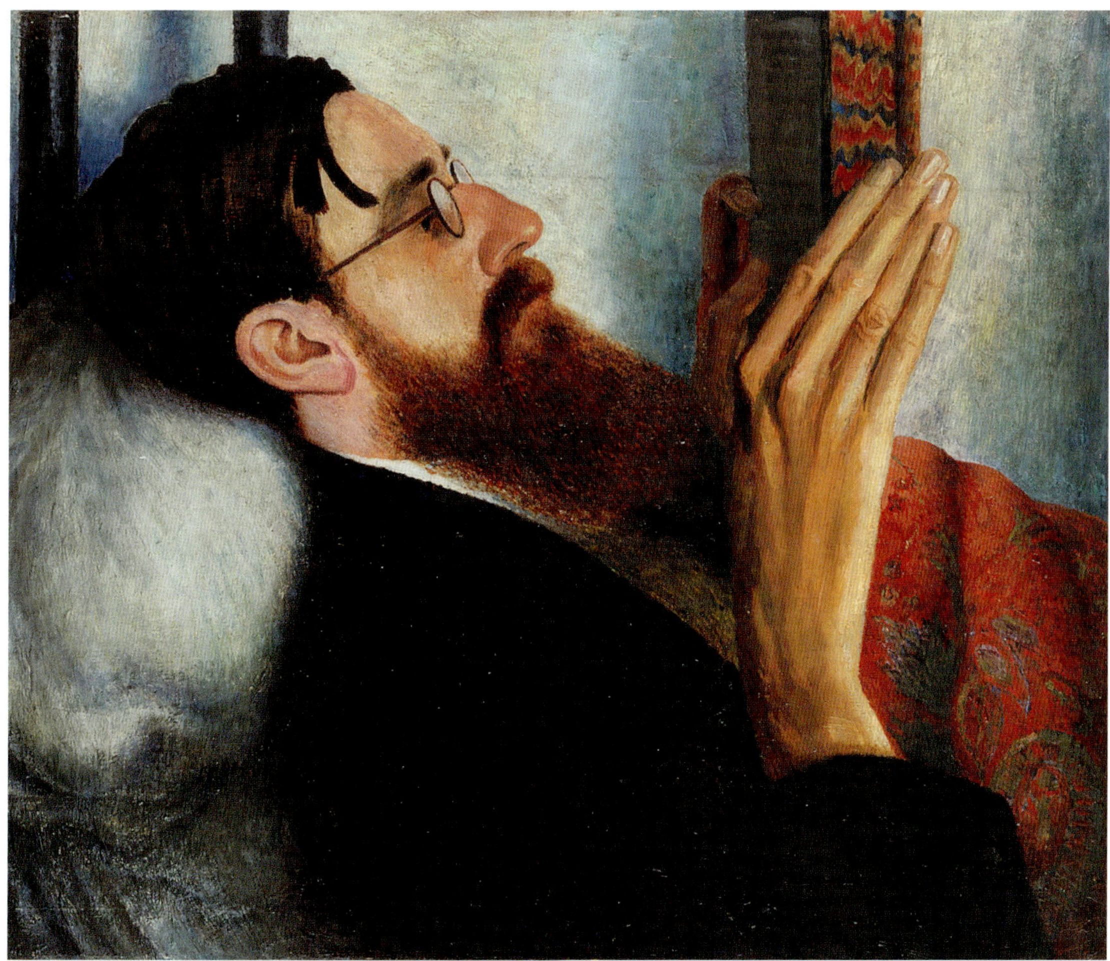

Lytton Strachey
Dora Carrington (1893–1932)
Oil on panel, 1916
508 x 609mm
NPG 6662

Lytton Strachey (1880–1932) was a central figure
in the Bloomsbury Group, and, as a celebrated
biographer and literary critic, his intellect was
an important element of the rarefied and often
irreverent atmosphere cultivated by its members.
Strachey studied (1899–1905) at Trinity College,
Cambridge, and his friendship with Leonard Woolf,
Clive Bell and Thoby Stephen formed the nucleus
of Bloomsbury. Strachey's first book, *Landmarks in
French Literature*, was published in 1912, and he wrote
numerous reviews for various journals, including the
Spectator and *Nation & Athenaeum*. His biographical
essays, *Eminent Victorians* (1918), made his name and
set new standards in biography, supplanting Victorian
hagiography with an approach that illuminated,
rather than explained, lives. Strachey met Dora
Carrington during the First World War and, when this
portrait was painted, he was a conscientious objector.
They lived together from 1917 until Strachey's death.
Devoted to Strachey, Carrington shot herself seven
weeks later.

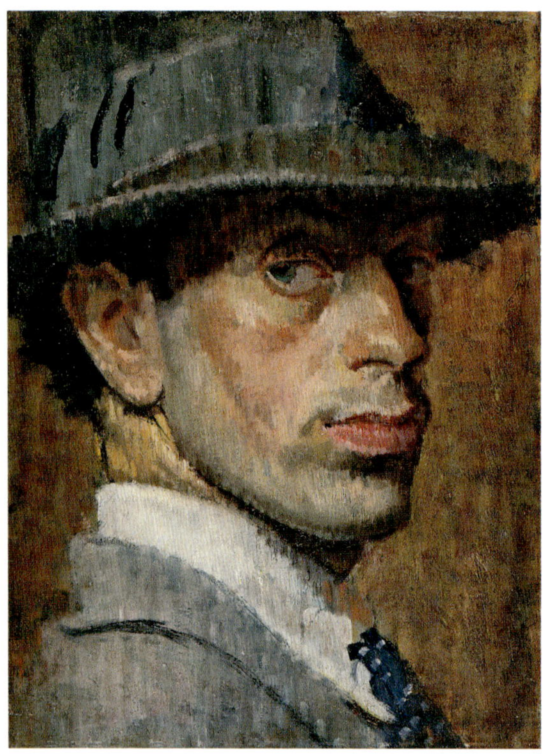

Isaac Rosenberg
Self-portrait
Oil on panel, 1915
295 x 222mm
NPG 4129

Artist and poet Isaac Rosenberg (1890–1918) was born in Bristol and moved to London with his family in 1897. He began writing poetry while an engravers' apprentice, work that he hated. Having completed his apprenticeship, he studied at the Slade School of Fine Art, where he came to know the painters Mark Gertler, David Bomberg, C.R.W. Nevinson and Stanley Spencer. His first collection of poems, *Night and Day*, was published in 1912. He also hoped to earn a living by painting portraits but, unable to afford sitters, he painted several self-portraits; his landscapes and allegorical scenes were exhibited at the Whitechapel Gallery in 1914. This self-portrait was painted in 1915, the year Rosenberg enlisted in the army. He depicted himself wearing a trilby, then fashionable among artists as a way of declaring their emancipated social status. Some of Rosenberg's best poems were written while serving on the Western Front, where he was killed on night patrol.

Vanessa Bell
Duncan Grant (1885–1978)
Oil on canvas, *c*.1918
940 x 606mm
NPG 4331

The painter Vanessa Bell (1879–1961) was the elder sister of Virginia Woolf. Following the death in 1904 of their father, the literary historian Lesley Stephen, the 'at homes' the two sisters held at 46 Gordon Square became the focus of the Bloomsbury Group. In 1907, Vanessa married the art critic Clive Bell and, although they remained associated, she had affairs with the critic and painter Roger Fry and the artist Duncan Grant. Fry's involvement with French Post-Impressionism was an important influence both on Vanessa and Grant. After seeing the two important exhibitions of Post-Impressionism that Fry organised in 1910–11 and 1912, both Vanessa and Grant incorporated brighter colour and reductive abstraction within their work. Bell went on to paint some of the first abstract paintings in Britain. Her relationship with Grant dates from 1913, and this vibrant portrait celebrates their shared feeling for rich colour, in both art and dress. Having declared that 'elegance is becoming tiresome', she complained that people stared at her because of the bold colours of her clothes.

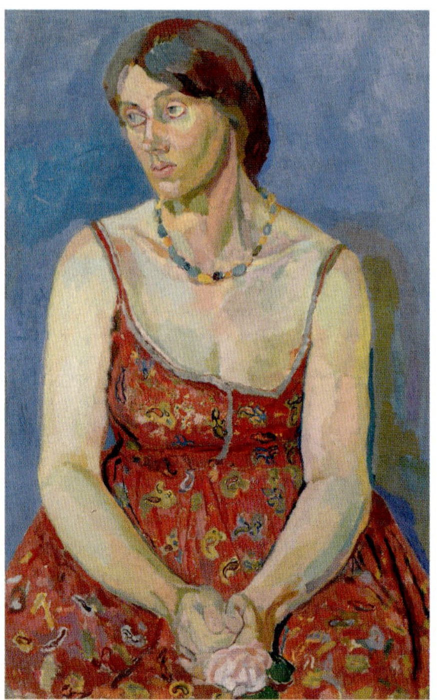

Sir John William Alcock
Ambrose McEvoy (1878–1927)
Oil on canvas, 1919
1499 x 1016mm
NPG 1894

On 14–15 June 1919, the aviator Sir John Alcock
(1892–1919), with Arthur Whitten Brown as navigator,
made the first non-stop flight across the Atlantic. This
feat, celebrated by McEvoy's portrait, was accomplished
in a converted Vickers Vimy bomber and took 16 hours
27 minutes. It secured Alcock and Brown a prize of
£10,000 from the *Daily Mail*, the owner of which, Lord
Northcliffe, was a keen advocate of aviation. By 1919,
a continuous air crossing of the Atlantic had become a
matter of hotly contested prestige. Previous attempts
had been interrupted by stops en route or ended in
failure. Alcock and Brown's mission was not without
its problems and hazards. An exhaust pipe ruptured,
radio contact was lost, navigation was impeded by dense
cloud, and the formation of ice was a constant threat to
the aircraft's controls. Northcliffe described the successful
crossing as 'a typical example of British courage and
organising efficiency'. McEvoy's portrait was timely.
Alcock died on 18 December 1919 in a flying accident
when he became trapped in fog and crash-landed.

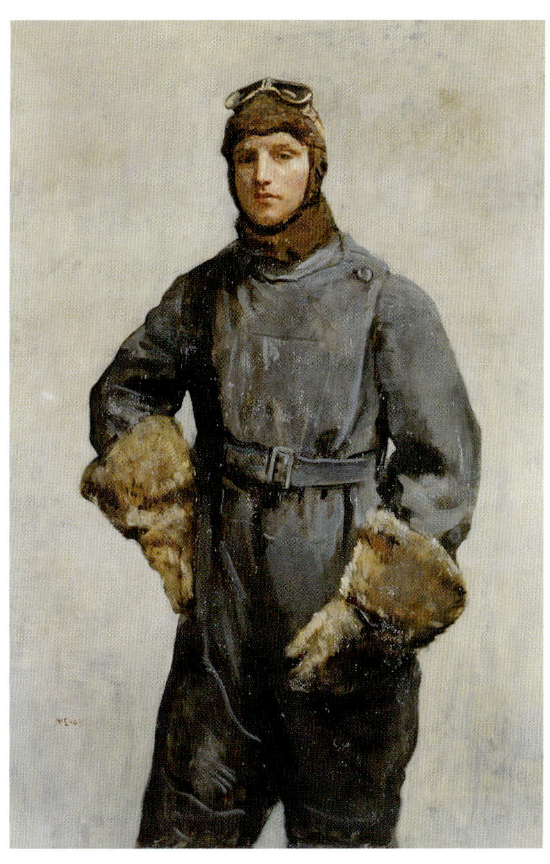

Radclyffe Hall
Charles Buchel (1872–1950)
Oil on canvas, 1918
914 x 711mm
NPG 4347

The author Radclyffe Hall (1880–1943) achieved
notoriety when her fifth novel, *The Well of Loneliness*
(1928), caused outrage and was banned. The book
was largely autobiographical and described a lesbian
relationship involving a female character, 'Stephen',
who dressed in masculine clothes. At a time when
male homosexuality was illegal, a government
official described the novel as 'inherently obscene
… it supports a depraved practice'. A self-professed
'congenital invert', Hall believed she was a man
inhabiting a woman's body. She cultivated a male
appearance, liked to be called John, and from 1918 lived
with another woman who became Hall's 'wife'. Buchel's
portrait dates from the beginning of that relationship.
It depicts Hall wearing a black jacket, cravat and a grey
skirt. This costume is deliberately unconventional yet
not exceptional among progressively minded women
of the time.

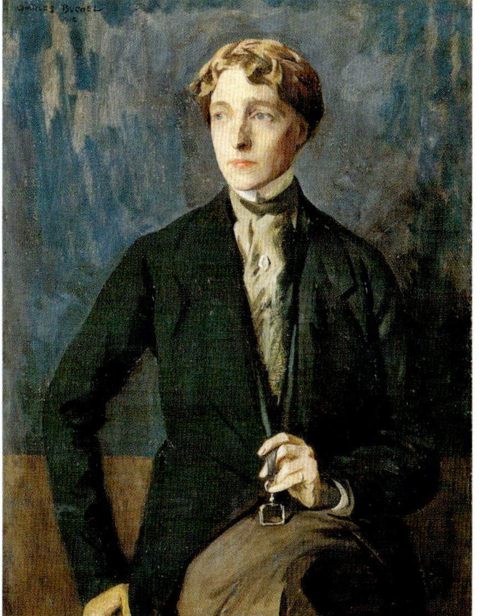

Sir Oswald Mosley
Glyn Warren Philpot (1884–1937)
Oil on canvas, 1925
762 x 636mm
NPG L184

Sir Oswald Mosley (1896–1980) was the political leader
of the British Union of Fascists (BUF), the movement he
launched in 1932. He was also one of the greatest public
speakers of the twentieth century. Philpot's portrait
shows Mosley the year after he joined the Labour
Party in 1924. After an outstanding parliamentary
performance in 1930, when as chancellor of the duchy
of Lancaster he resigned from the Labour Government,
for a while he was even seen as a future prime
minister. Mosley's formation of the BUF followed a
visit to Italy when he met Mussolini. Taking shape
against a background of economic catastrophe, the
BUF attracted followers. But the aggression showed
by Mosley's black-shirted stewards at a rally held at
Olympia in 1934, and the BUF's subsequent anti-
Semitism, alienated support. His opposition to conflict
with Germany also isolated him. After the declaration of
war in 1939 he maintained a peace campaign, but from
1940 to 1943 he was interned, his dream of fascism in
Britain at an end.

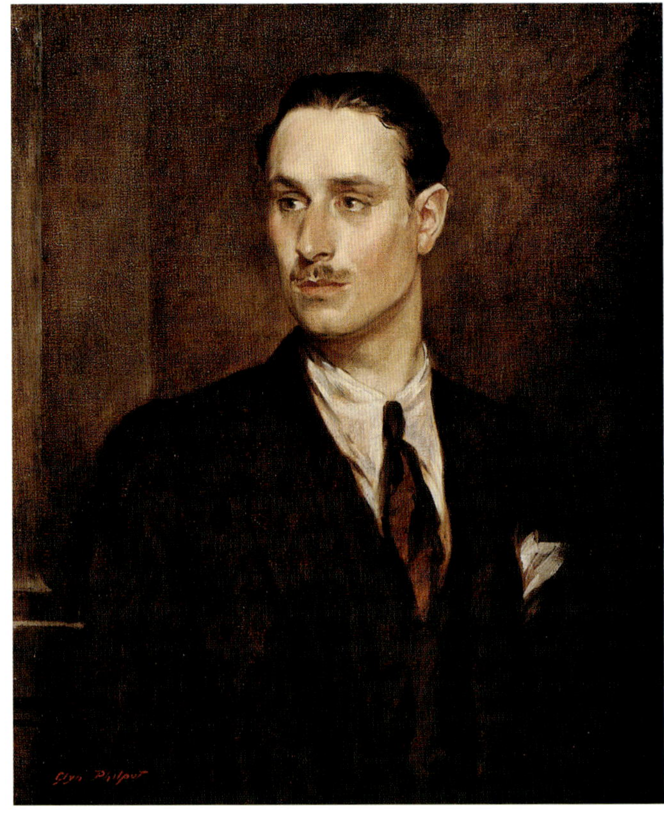

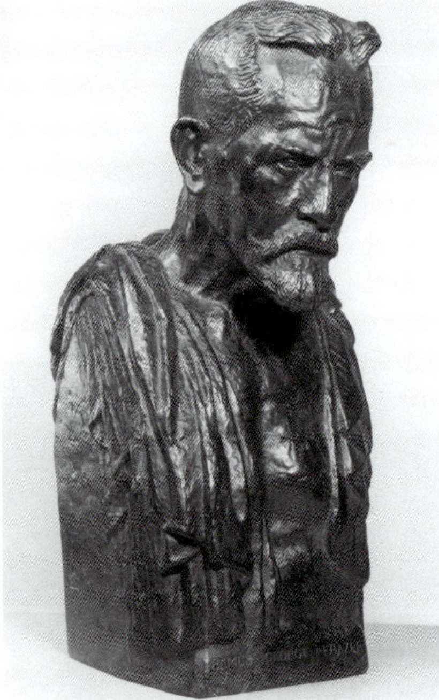

Sir James George Frazer
Emile-Antoine Bourdelle (1861–1929)
Bronze bust, 1925, cast of 1922 original
679mm high
NPG 2099

Social anthropologist and classical scholar Sir James
George Frazer (1854–1941) achieved fame for his multi-
volume work, *The Golden Bough*. First published in two
parts in 1890, the third edition of 1911–14 had grown
to twelve volumes. Drawing on a vast amount of data
relating to the religious beliefs and practices of earlier
cultures, Frazer's subject was the evolution of human
understanding through the successive phases of magic,
religion and science. Presenting religion as a stage in
evolution, Frazer can be seen as an important exponent
of secularism in the twentieth century. The one-volume
version (1922) sold tens of thousands of copies and had
a profound influence, many swayed by the implication
that Christianity was a remnant of a superseded outlook.
During the sitting for the bust made by Bourdelle,
Fraser neither moved nor spoke, saying he had the
impression that a masterpiece was being created.

Frederick Delius
Ernest Procter (1886–1935)
Oil on millboard, 1929
321 x 262mm
NPG 3861

The music of Bradford-born composer Frederick Delius
(1862–1934) was at times closely connected with the
English pastoral tradition, yet it transcends national
boundaries. He studied at the Leipzig Conservatory
(1886–8) and later, while living in Paris, belonged to a
circle that included Gauguin, Strindberg and Munch.
During the early years of the century his music achieved
prominence in Germany. After being championed by
Sir Thomas Beecham, Delius also found an audience in
Britain. *Brigg Fair*, *On Hearing the First Cuckoo in Spring*
and *North Country Sketches* evoke his attachment to
the English landscape and exemplify the atmospheric
character of Delius's style. By 1928 he had become
blind and paralysed, but continued to compose with
the assistance of a dedicated amanuensis, Eric Fenby.
Procter's portrait depicts the composer at a rehearsal
of his *A Mass of Life* in the Queen's Hall, London in
November 1929.

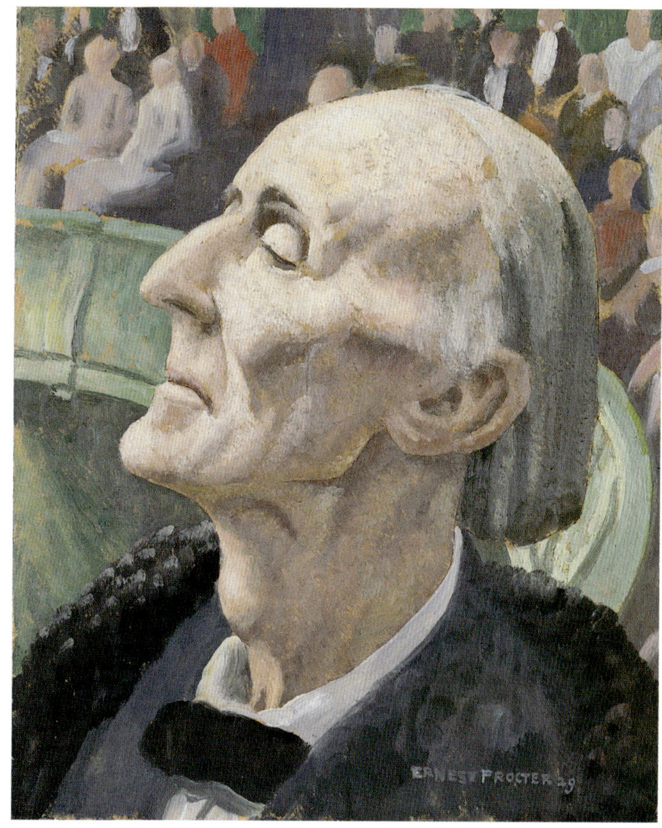

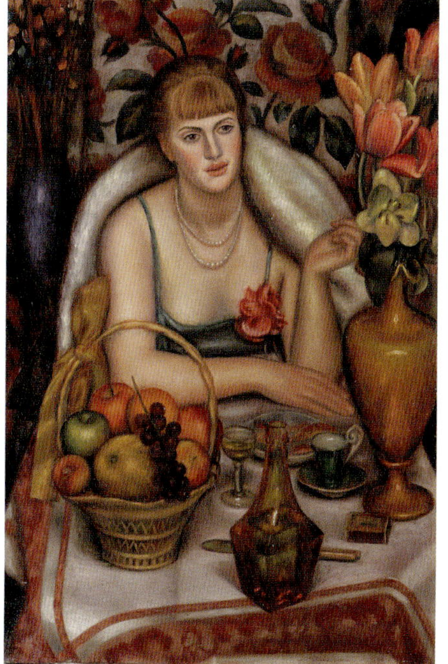

**Natalie Bevan (née Ackenhausen, later Denny,
Sieveking and Barclay)**
Mark Gertler (1891–1939)
Oil on canvas, 1928
1075 x 718mm
NPG 6877

Entitled *Supper*, Gertler's sensuous portrait of the
painter, ceramicist and artist's muse Natalie Bevan
(1909–2007) celebrates one of the most charismatic
women of her generation. From the late 1920s Bevan
became a popular figure in London's artistic milieu.
She sat for two portraits by Gertler after they met
at a party held by Augustus John. A regular at Soho's
Gargoyle Club, she was also connected with several
other artists including C.R.W. Nevinson, John Armstrong
and, later, Paul Nash. She married Bobby Bevan, the
son of Camden Town Group painters Robert Bevan and
Stanislawa de Karlowska, in 1946. A celebrated hostess,
their home, Boxted House on the Essex–Suffolk border,
became a showcase for their illustrious art collection
and an important gathering place for modern artists.
For many years *Supper* was displayed at Boxted House.

Dame Edith Sitwell
Maurice Lambert (1901–64)
Aluminium head, 1985, from the original, *c*.1926–7
354mm high
NPG 5801

Following a reading of her poem, *Façade*, in London's
Aeolian Hall in June 1923, Dame Edith Sitwell
(1887–1964) became the most discussed modernist
poets in England. Sister of the writers Sacheverell
and Osbert Sitwell, her first volume of poems was
published in 1915. As editor of *Wheels*, from 1916 to
1921, she encouraged avant-garde writers and aroused
considerable controversy among conservative critics.
Façade continued that confrontational stance.
Delivered with her back to the audience, it used rhythm
and rhyme to explore a world of sensory impressions.
Subsequently her brothers suggested that it be set to
music by William Walton. It was probably Osbert who
decided to commission this sculpture from Lambert,
having seen his work in a group exhibition in London in
1925. Unusually, it was cast in aluminium. Lambert later
included the head, of which this is a later cast, in his
first one-man exhibition in 1927.

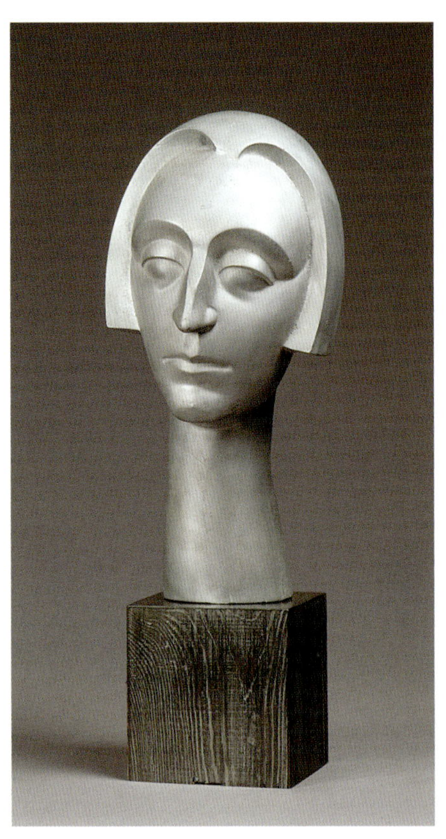

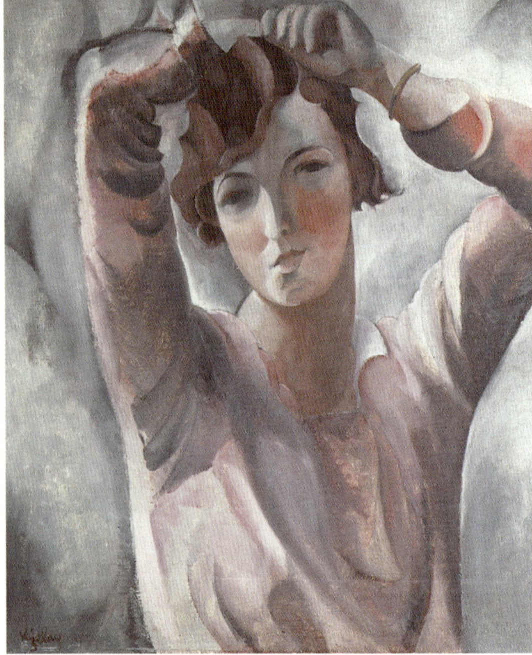

Paule Vézelay *(Harmony)*
Self-portrait
Oil on canvas, *c*.1927–9
651 x 543mm
NPG 6003

A member of the Paris-based Abstraction-Création
group from 1934, Paule Vézelay (1892–1984) was one
of the first British artists to commit fully to abstract
painting. Born Marjorie Watson-Williams, she studied
at Bristol School of Art (1909–12) and the London
School of Art (1912–14). Claiming that 'English art then
bored me to tears', her first solo exhibition was held in
1920 in Brussels, and from there she first visited Paris.
Following an interlude in London, in 1926 she settled
in Paris and adopted the name Paule Vézelay. Contact
with the leading modern artists in Paris, notably Matisse,
Miró, Kandinsky and Gris, and a relationship with the
surrealist painter André Masson, were vital influences.
By the mid-1930s, recognisable subject matter had
disappeared from Vézelay's painting. This self-portrait
was painted shortly after Vézelay moved to Paris.
Entitled *Harmony*, it demonstrates the artist's progression
towards abstracted form and non-naturalistic colour.

Sir Winston Churchill
Walter Richard Sickert (1860–1942)
Oil on canvas, 1927
457 x 305mm
NPG 4438

This portrait of Sir Winston Churchill
(1874–1965), who would later
become British prime minister and
Britain's greatest war-time leader,
was painted when he was Chancellor
of the Exchequer in Stanley Baldwin's
administration of 1924–9. Sickert was
a friend of Churchill's mother-in-law,
Lady Blanche Hozier. Also, Churchill's
wife Clementine, as a child, had known
the artist in Dieppe. At the time it was
painted, Churchill, an amateur painter,
was receiving lessons from Sickert.
In common with his usual practice,
Sickert used photographs as the basis
for the portrait, although it was also
partly based on observation from life.
A squared-up drawing, possibly made
from photographs, was used to trace the
image on to the canvas. The distinctive
underpainting in cobalt and pink relates
to the method described by Sickert in
letters to the sitter. Despite its complex
and careful gestation, Churchill disliked
the portrait. Churchill's own paintings
are housed at his family home, Chartwell
in Kent, which is owned by the National
Trust.

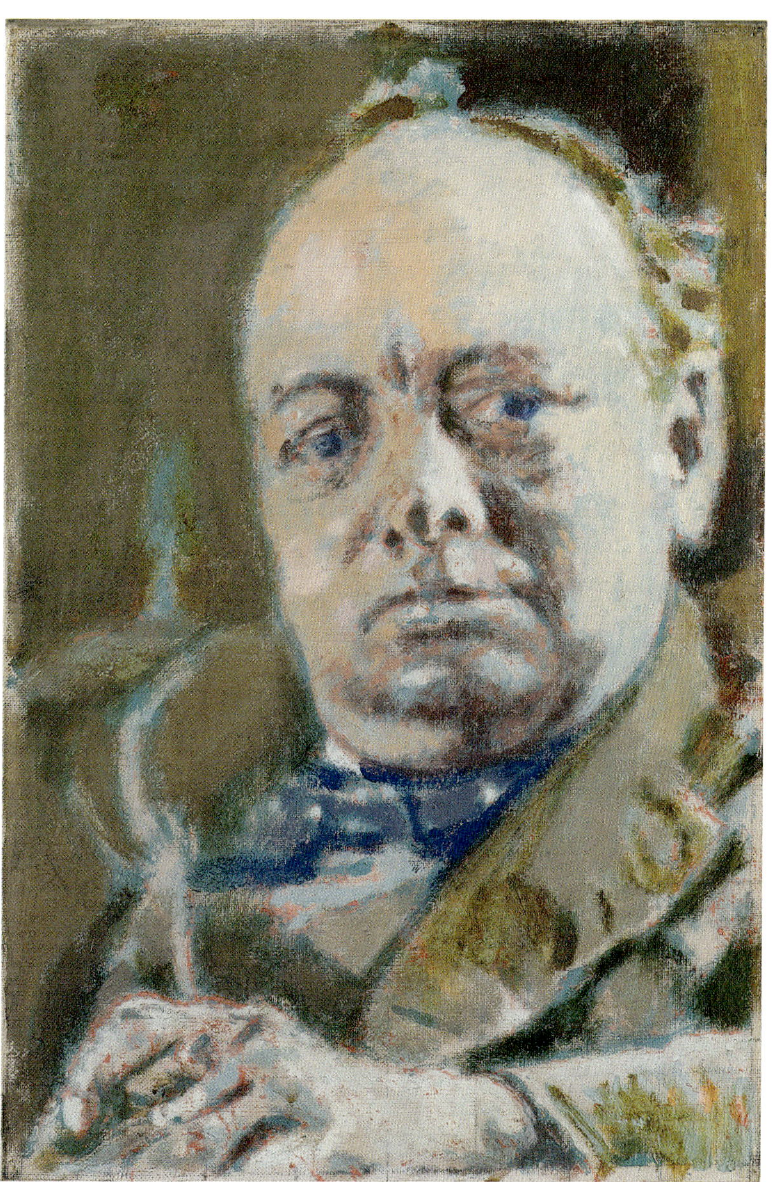

Interlude and storm

During the 1930s, the seeds of instability sown by the First World War sent up shoots that penetrated cracks in the social order. On the international stage, Hitler's appointment as chancellor of Germany in 1933, and his subsequent introduction of conscription, were worrying developments. In Britain, economic recession, strikes and mass unemployment put a brake on progress and recovery. In 1936, King George V died and was succeeded by Edward VIII who, within months, abdicated.

In the visual arts, modernism persisted but, with exceptions, this existed mainly at the periphery. Gabo, Mondrian and Kokoschka all came to England and made an important but largely invisible impression. Ben Nicholson, whose arresting double portrait with Barbara Hepworth was made in 1933, was connected with Unit One, a short-lived progressive association of artists that exhibited in 1934. Throughout the inter-war years, Sir Herbert Read, whose portrait was later painted by Patrick Heron (see p.7), championed avant-garde art in Britain.

In 1936, Surrealism found a British audience when the International Surrealist Exhibition was held in London. It included John Banting, whose 1934 portrait of the photographer Humphrey Spender is notable. Between 1937 and 1938 Spender worked for the important Mass Observation movement, which aimed to document the everyday lives of ordinary people in Britain.

The modernist architect Ernö Goldfinger, who came to London in 1934, was also closely associated with British Surrealism and sat for a portrait by Eileen Agar. Despite economic depression, portraiture flourished during the 1930s, supported by commissions and embracing both progressive and more conservative, homegrown tendencies.

On 3 September 1939, Britain and France responded to German aggression in Europe by declaring war. Yousuf Karsh's magisterial photographic portrait of Sir Winston Churchill, made in 1941, depicts Britain's prime minister who, throughout the conflict, was an inspiring leader.

Sir Winston Churchill
Yousuf Karsh (1908–2002)
Bromide print, 1941
277 x 217mm
NPG P490 (16)

Yousuf Karsh's portrait of Britain's prime
minister during the Second World War
is one of the most reproduced images
in the history of photography. Prior to
the declaration of war in September
1939, Sir Winston Churchill (1874–1965)
had opposed appeasement with
Hitler. In 1940 he challenged Neville
Chamberlain's leadership and succeeded
him, telling the nation, 'I have nothing
to offer but blood, toil, tears and sweat.'
Working with other world leaders,
including Roosevelt, de Gaulle and
Stalin, his inspirational presence saw
Britain through its deepest crisis. Karsh
photographed Churchill during a visit
to the Canadian House of Commons
in Ottawa in 1941. Snatching the cigar
from the mouth of the 'roaring lion',
as Churchill was dubbed, Karsh recalled
'he looked so belligerent he could have
devoured me.' Capturing that expression,
the photograph's subsequent success
elevated Karsh's reputation to the
highest rank.

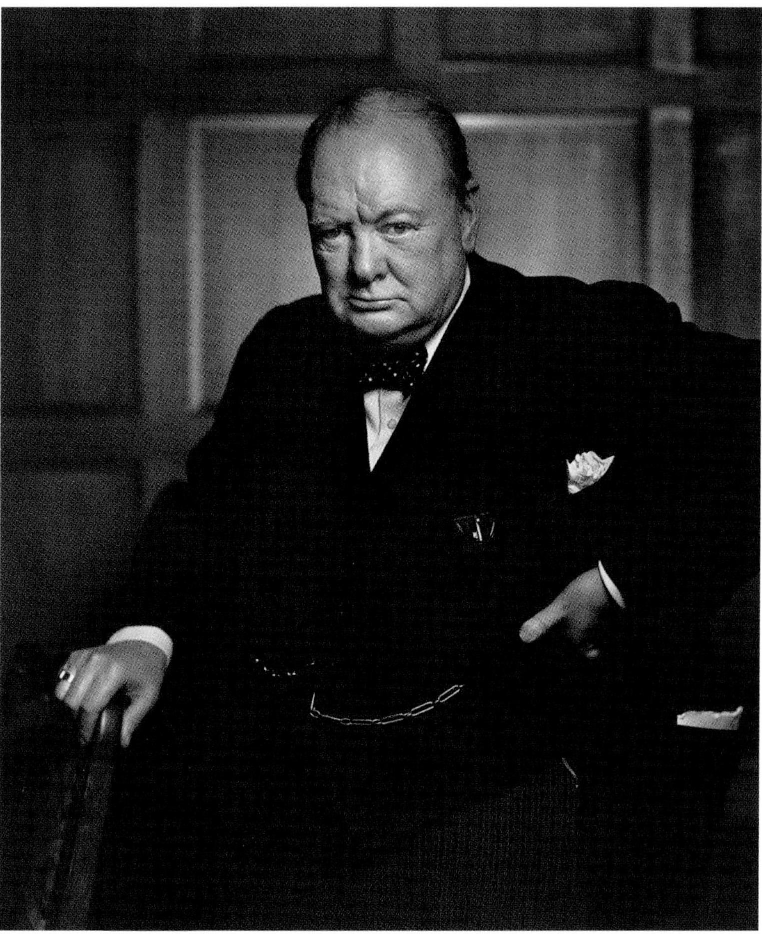

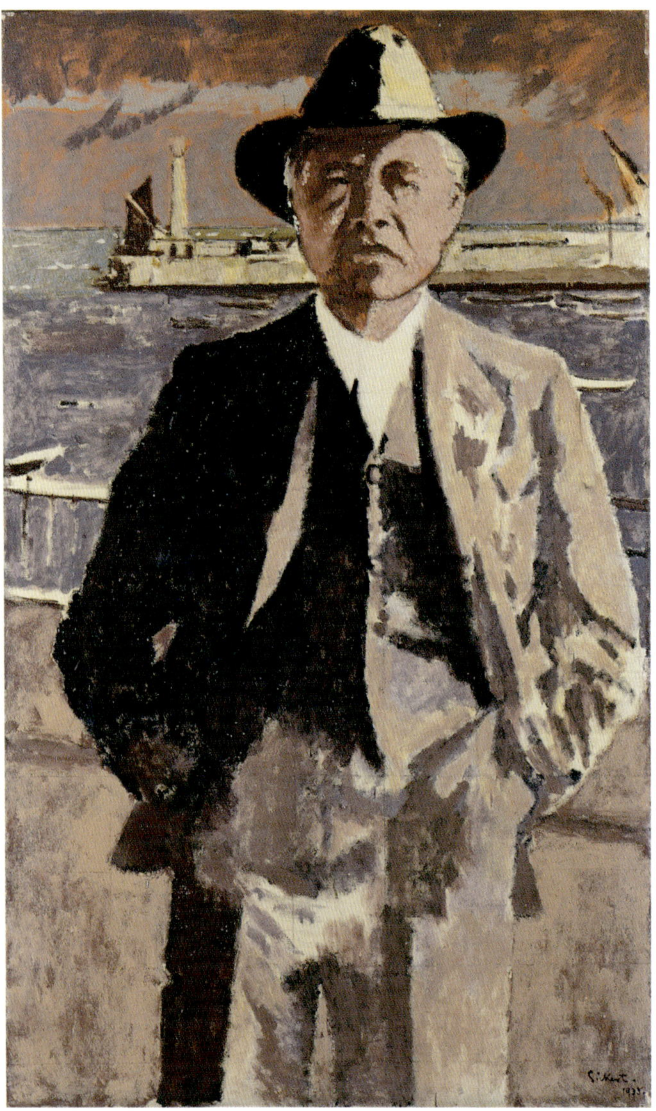

William Maxwell Aitken, 1st Baron Beaverbrook
Walter Richard Sickert (1860–1942)
Oil on canvas, 1935
1762 x 1073mm
NPG 5173

Newspaper proprietor and politician
Baron Beaverbrook (1879–1964) was
a prominent and influential figure in
British public life. Elected a Conservative
MP in 1910, he rarely spoke in the
House of Commons, but his actions
as a go-between helped Lloyd George
supersede Asquith as British prime
minister in 1916. Beaverbrook became
the first Minister of Information in 1918,
responsible for Allied propaganda. A love
of journalism led to his acquiring a string
of newspapers, including the *Sunday
Express* in 1918 and the *Evening Standard*
in 1923. During the 1936 abdication
crisis, he backed Edward VIII in his
attempt to retain the throne. Sickert's
portrait was painted from an informal
snapshot of Beaverbrook, taken on the
veranda of his country home in Surrey.
Sickert replaced the background with a
more dramatic view depicting Margate
harbour. Although the Royal Academy
rejected the portrait for the 1935
Summer Exhibition, Sickert considered
it one of his 'best and most important
works'.

Ben Nicholson and Barbara Hepworth
***1933 (St Rémy – self-portrait with
Barbara Hepworth)***
Ben Nicholson (1894–1982)
Oil on canvas, 1933
273 x 168mm
NPG 5591

Ben Nicholson was the leading British
abstract artist of his generation. Son of
the painters William Nicholson and
Mabel Pryde, he attended (1910–11) the
Slade School of Fine Art. In 1924 he
joined the 7 and 5 Society. Founded in
1919, the original group of seven painters
and five sculptors grew to become
the main association of progressive
British artists until the early Thirties.
The sculptor Barbara Hepworth
(1903–75), depicted with Nicholson
in this double portrait, was elected in
1932. Subsequently both artists joined
the avant-garde group Unit One.
Nicholson had met Hepworth in 1931.
In that year they exhibited together and
in 1932 travelled to France, where they
made contact with Arp, Brancusi and
Picasso. They began sharing a studio
in Hampstead, London, around this
time. Their relationship is celebrated in
this portrait, which superimposes their
profiles using abstracted, fluid shapes
and lines reminiscent of the Surrealist
painter Joan Miró. They married in 1934.

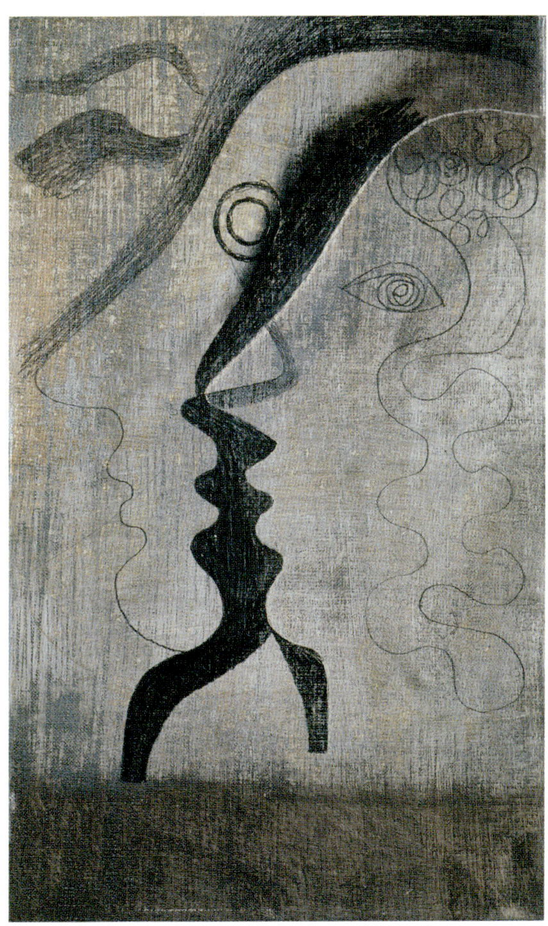

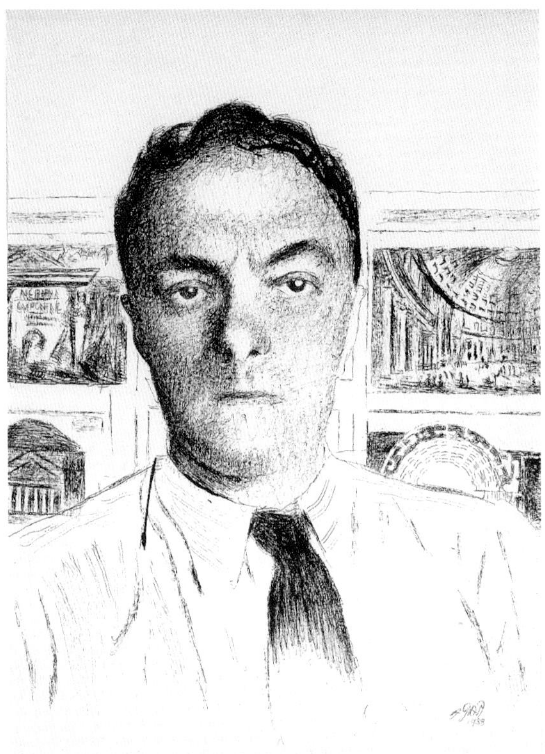

Ernö Goldfinger
Eileen Agar (1899–1991)
Pen and ink, 1938
524 x 394mm
NPG 6099

Born in Budapest, the modernist architect Ernö
Goldfinger (1902–87) studied in Paris and in 1934
settled in London. Following that move he became one
of the principal links between British and Continental
architecture. From 1934 to 1974, he was the British
correspondent of *L'Architecture d'Aujourdhui* and
co-founded the International Union of Architects.
In London an early success was Willow Road.
The building comprises a row of three houses,
overlooking Hampstead Heath, built between
1937 and 1940. In that building's clean, essential
lines, Goldfinger articulated the ethos of 'structural
rationalism' that defined his approach. One of the
three houses is now owned by the National Trust and
contains Goldfinger's modern art collection among
other possessions. He later became known for his
1960s office blocks, notably Alexander Fleming House,
built for the Ministry of Health, and multi-storey
housing. In the face of later criticism, he was a staunch
advocate of the tower block. Goldfinger was linked
with several artists associated with the Surrealist
movement, including Max Ernst, Roland Penrose,
Lee Miller and Eileen Agar, who drew this portrait.

King George V
Sir Oswald Birley (1880–1952)
Oil on canvas, *c*.1933
591 x 429mm
NPG 4013

King George V (1865–1936) was the second son of
Edward VII and Queen Alexandra. His elder brother
having died in 1892, George succeeded to the throne
in 1910. Though no intellectual, he had an exceptional
memory for detail and conducted his reign with a
steady sense of responsibility. George V was faced with a
succession of crises, including a bill to curb the House
of Lords, the conflicts relating to Irish Home Rule,
the First World War and, during the post-war period,
great political and social upheaval. Throughout, he
smoothed the process of change with a non-partisan
approach. However, his attitude to the visual arts was
conservative. He laughed at Impressionist paintings
and shook his stick at a painting by Cézanne.
His introduction of a royal Christmas radio broadcast
in 1932 enlarged the monarchy's contact with its
subjects, and his death provoked national and imperial
mourning. Birley's sympathetic portrait captures
something of the King's traditional manner during
turbulent times.

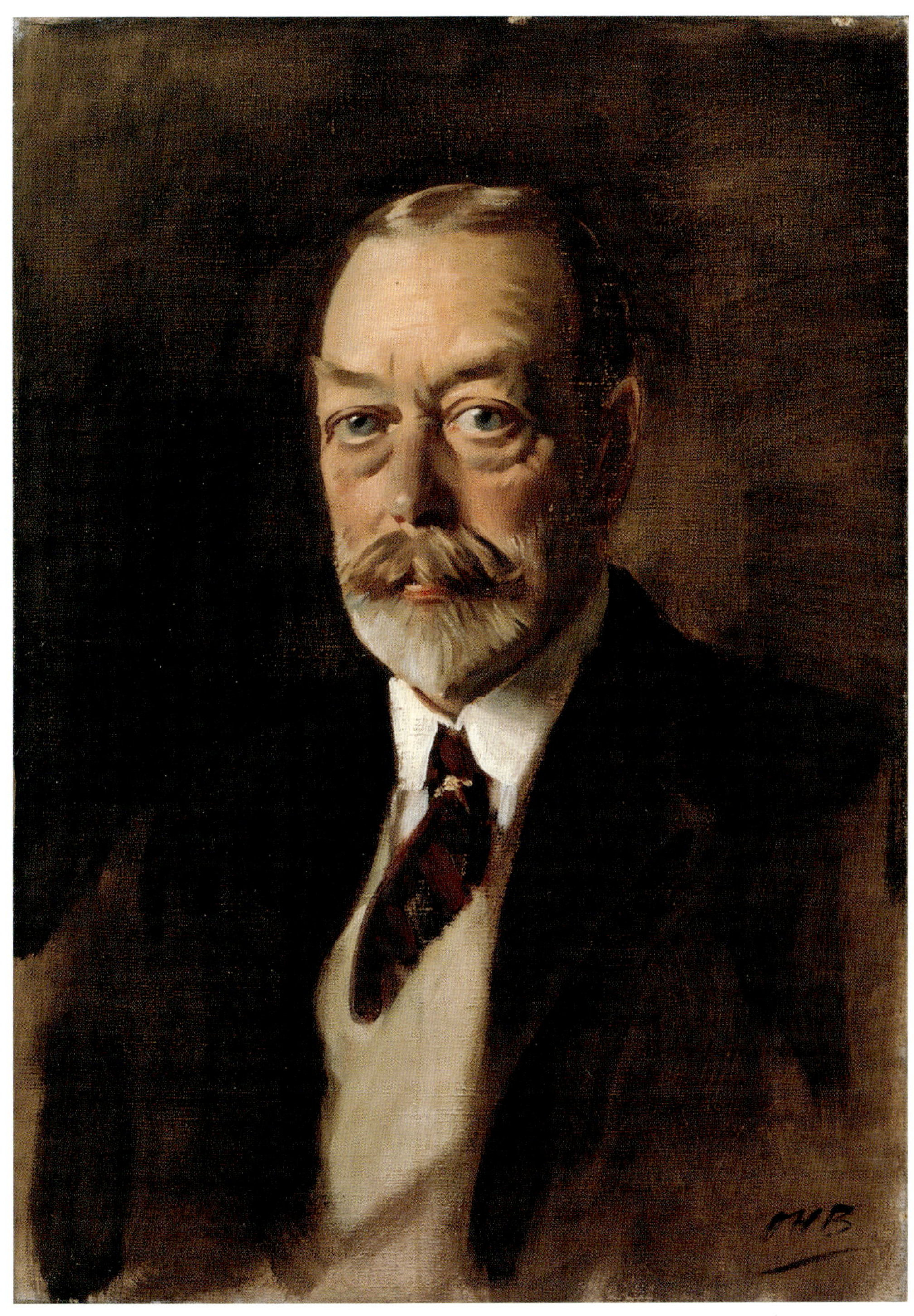

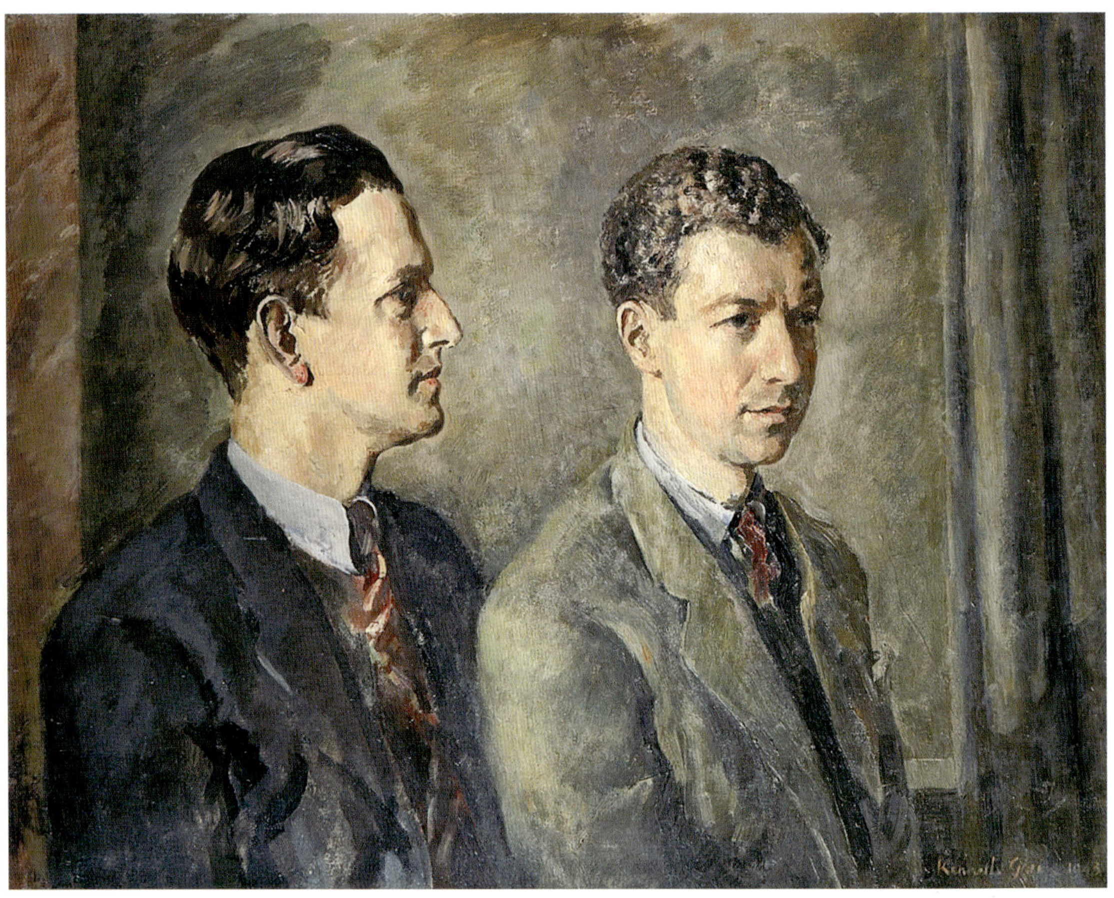

Peter Pears and Benjamin Britten
Kenneth Green (1905–86)
Oil on canvas, 1943
715 x 969mm
NPG 5136

The immediate success of Benjamin Britten's opera *Peter Grimes* in 1945 brought the composer international recognition, unprecedented in British music. Britten's subsequent compositions in that genre, and also his *War Requiem* (1961), which had a worldwide impact, confirmed his position as one of the twentieth century's leading composers of vocal music. In addition, Britten (1913–76) made a profound contribution to non-vocal genres, notably numerous chamber works and pieces for orchestra. The tenor Peter Pears (1910–86), who was Britten's partner from the late 1930s, created the title roles in thirteen of Britten's operas. With writer Eric Crozier, they founded the Aldeburgh Festival in 1948. Kenneth Green's double portrait depicts the two men in 1943, the year that Britten composed his *Serenade* for tenor, horn and strings. Both were conscientious objectors, Britten's exemption being granted on condition that he gave concerts with Pears for the wartime Committee for the Encouragement of Music and the Arts.

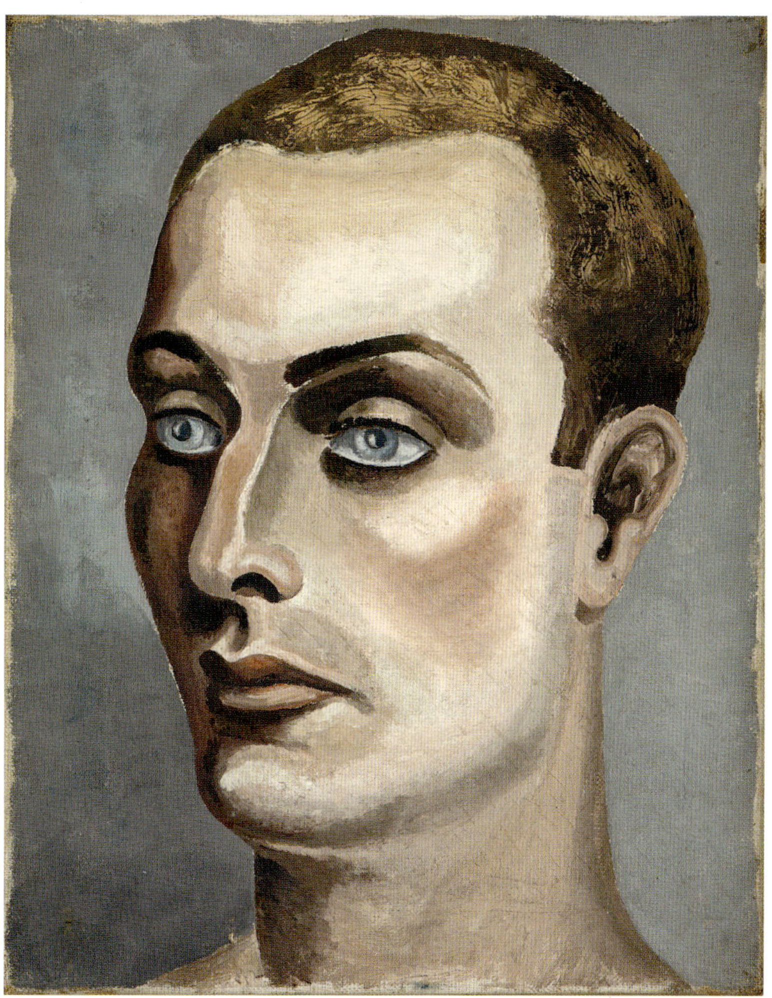

Humphrey Spender
John Banting (1902–72)
Oil on canvas, *c.*1934
381 x 304mm
NPG 6922

Photographer, artist and designer Humphrey Spender (1910–2005) studied art history at the University of Freiburg and later trained as an architect. However, his earlier contact in Germany with European avant-garde photography and film drew him to photojournalism. In 1935 he worked for a while for the *Daily Mirror*. Later he travelled in Germany with his brother the writer Stephen Spender and Christopher Isherwood, for whose book, *Goodbye to Berlin* (1939), he designed the cover. As a leading member of the Mass Observation movement, Spender took hundreds of photographs, his work documenting an era in British social history that has now vanished. His subjects included street scenes, public houses, sports and leisure pursuits. In Bolton alone, he took 900 photographs, which provide a vivid insight into life in a pre-war British industrial town. Banting, who was a close friend, was connected with British Surrealism.

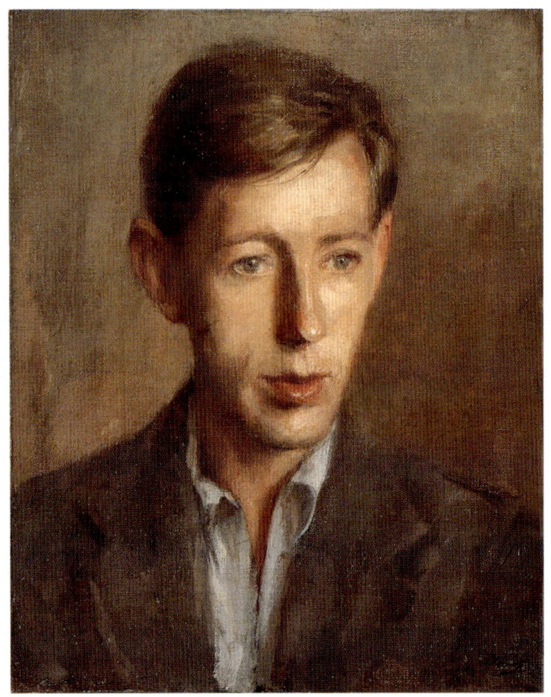

Laurie Lee
Anthony Devas (1911–58)
Oil on canvas, 1944
508 x 410mm
NPG 6726

Although Laurie Lee (1914–97) preferred to think of
himself as a poet, his literary reputation rests on
his autobiographical trilogy, *Cider with Rosie* (1959),
As I Walked Out One Midsummer Morning (1969) and
A Moment of War (1991). Each book blends personal
reminiscence with an acute sense of time and place.
Cider with Rosie evokes the writer's Cotswold childhood
in the wake of the First World War, a period that saw
'the end of a thousand years' life'. After travelling in
Spain during the Civil War, Lee lived in London. He first
gained recognition for the poems he published from 1941.
His debut volume of poetry, *The Sun My Monument*,
appeared in 1944, the year that Devas painted this
portrait. Lee was then a lodger with the painter in his
Chelsea house, and his circle of literary friends included
Stephen Spender, Cecil Day-Lewis and John and
Rosamond Lehmann.

James Joyce
Jacques-Emile Blanche (1861–1942)
Oil on canvas, 1935
1251 x 876mm
NPG 3883

Until 1936, the year after Blanche completed this
portrait of James Joyce (1882–1941), the Irish
novelist's most celebrated book, *Ulysses*, was banned
in Britain. The novel that followed in 1939, *Finnegans
Wake*, was the product of seventeen years' labour,
and its formidable obscurity mark it as one of modern
literature's most challenging works. Joyce was born in
Dublin, where he later studied. From 1905, he lived in
Vienna, Prague and Zurich, and from 1920 in Paris.
With *Ulysses*, his great experiment in style, he introduced
an unprecedented realism to the novel. Blanche's
portrait is contemporaneous with Sickert's painting
of Beaverbrook, but the divergence in styles is telling,
the former being more conservative. Ironically, the
French artist was accused by critics in his own country
of plagiarising Reynolds, Gainsborough and Lawrence.
In Britain, where such connections with the past were
welcomed, Blanche's approach was accepted. Joyce was
self-conscious about the heavy lenses in his spectacles
and asked the artist to depict him from the side.

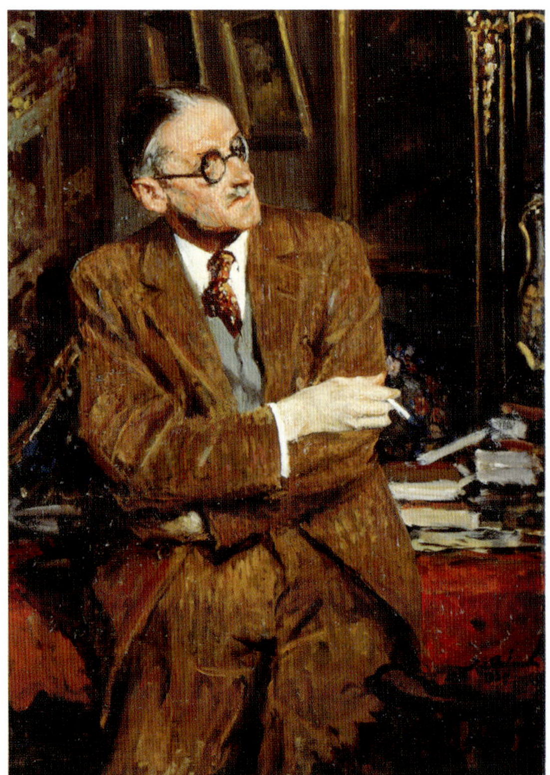

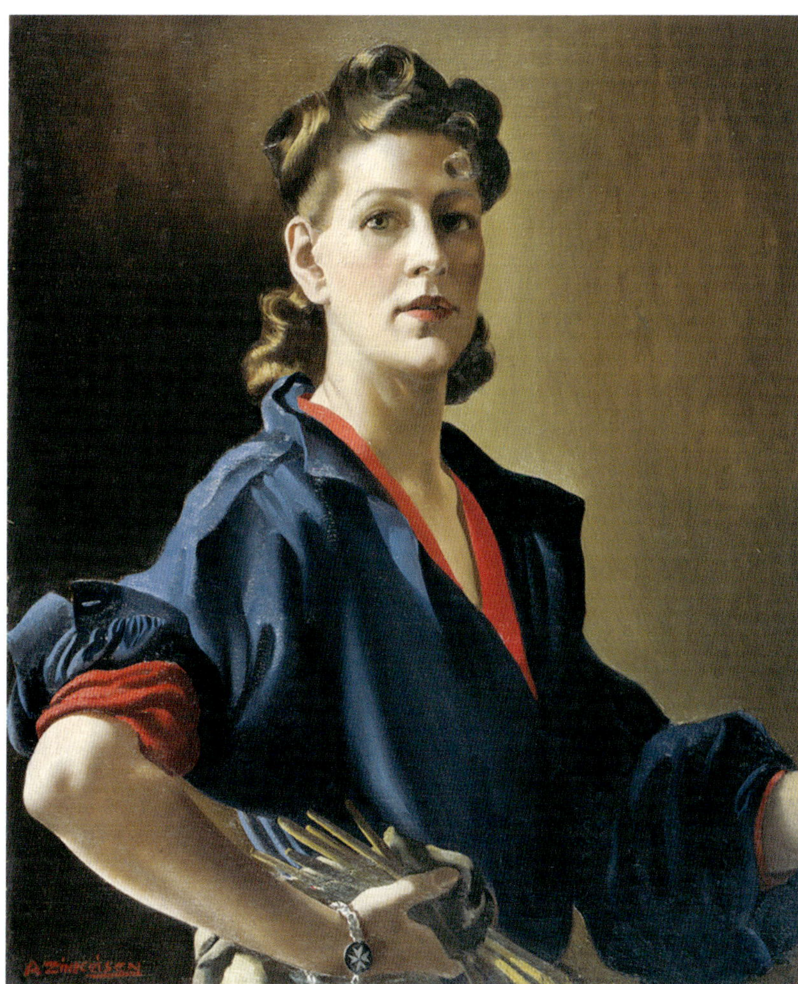

Anna Zinkeisen
Self-portrait
Oil on canvas, *c.*1944
752 x 625mm
NPG 5884

Painter of portraits, still lifes, murals and landscapes, Anna Zinkeisen (1901–76) exemplifies those traditional values of fidelity to observation and meticulous draughtsmanship that endured in Britain, especially prior to 1945, alongside more avant-garde trends. Having trained at the Royal Academy Schools, she exhibited there from 1921 to 1964. She also made designs for magazine covers, book jackets and advertisements and, during the inter-war period, undertook commissioned murals for the ocean liners *Queen Mary* and *Queen Elizabeth*. As a medical artist at St Mary's Hospital, Paddington, in the Second World War, she documented the injuries and operations connected with civilian bombing. Although painted at that time, and possibly in the disused operating theatre she used as a studio, there is no trace of privation or uncertainty in Zinkeisen's self-portrait. The coiffure, make-up and enamelled bracelet bearing the insignia of St John Ambulance, all convey assurance and purpose.

Transition

As had been the case from 1914 to 1918, the Second World War struck at the very foundations of Western society. In addition to the huge loss of human life, both military and civilian, an even darker shadow was cast by new, ominous developments. In 1945, the war against Japan was ended when atomic bombs were dropped on two cities, Hiroshima and Nagasaki, with devastating consequences. In 1946, the Nuremberg trials of defeated Nazis brought to light the full horror of the Holocaust, in which an estimated six million Jews and others subjected to persecution were murdered. It seemed that an unexpected, disturbing aspect of human nature had been exposed.

One consequence of the sense that the world had changed was to open the door to new means of artistic expression. Tradition now seemed less relevant in an age whose values had been overturned. In Britain, the leading literary figure of the post-war period was the modernist poet T.S. Eliot, whose abstracted portrait by Patrick Heron was painted after Eliot was awarded the Noble Prize in Literature in 1948. Eliot's *Four Quartets*, published in 1943, set the tone of disaster, and, although that was his last major work of poetry, he continued to be an influential cultural and literary critic. In 1953, Queen Elizabeth II was crowned. As portrayed by the photographer Dorothy Wilding, her youthful radiance illuminated a nation then still subject to food rationing.

In the visual arts, the formation of the Arts Council in 1946 provided official support for more progressive approaches, and this led to a growing acceptance of modern art. The Festival of Britain in 1951 showcased work by, among others, Francis Bacon, Lucian Freud, Graham Sutherland, Rodrigo Moynihan and Ruskin Spear, all of whom subsequently entered the National Portrait Gallery's Collection, either as artist or sitter. In some portraits of that time the immediate consequence was a growing informality, as is evident in the c.1952 painting of Eduardo Paolozzi by Cathleen Mann and that of Kingsley Amis by Gordon Stuart in 1953. For some, this more direct approach was unwelcome. Sutherland's 1954 portrait of Churchill, which was commissioned to mark the statesman's eightieth birthday, was disliked by the sitter and was later destroyed. A study survives.

Queen Elizabeth II
Dorothy Wilding (1893–1976)
Chlorobromide print on tissue and card
mount, 1952
290 x 215mm
NPG P870(5)

Queen Elizabeth II (b.1926) acceded
to the throne at the age of twenty-five,
following the death of her father George
VI on 6 February 1952. This celebrated
photograph is one of fifty-nine
portraits taken to mark her accession.
Significantly, the focus is on her youth,
freshness and glamour, qualities that
enlivened a nation even then recovering
from the effects of the war and still
subject to food rationing. The monarch
is shown wearing the English rose
diamond necklace that was a wedding
gift from the Nizam of Hyderabad and
an elegant evening dress by Norman
Hartnell. Copies of this portrait were
sent to embassies around the world, and
it also formed the basis for banknote
and stamp design. It thus played a
significant part in disseminating the
Queen's image at a crucial moment
in her reign. Celebrated for her society
photographs, it appears that Dorothy
Wilding did not herself take this famous
photograph: she entrusted the task to
an assistant, adding her signature to
the result.

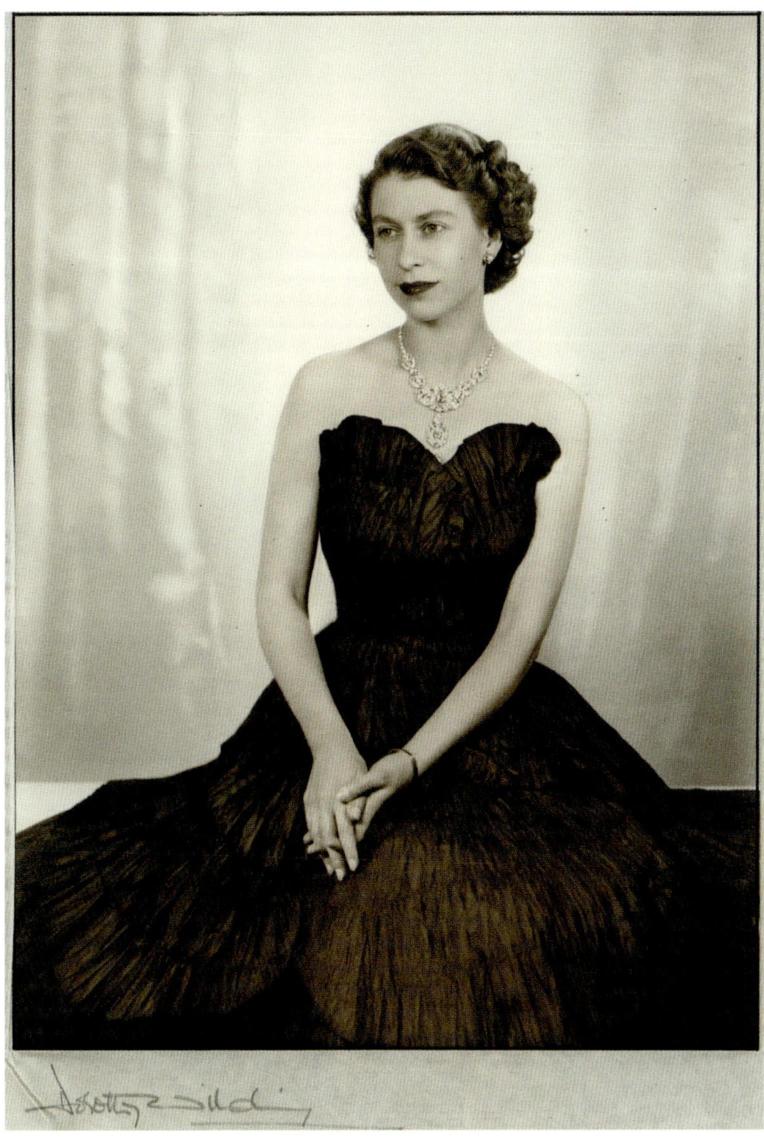

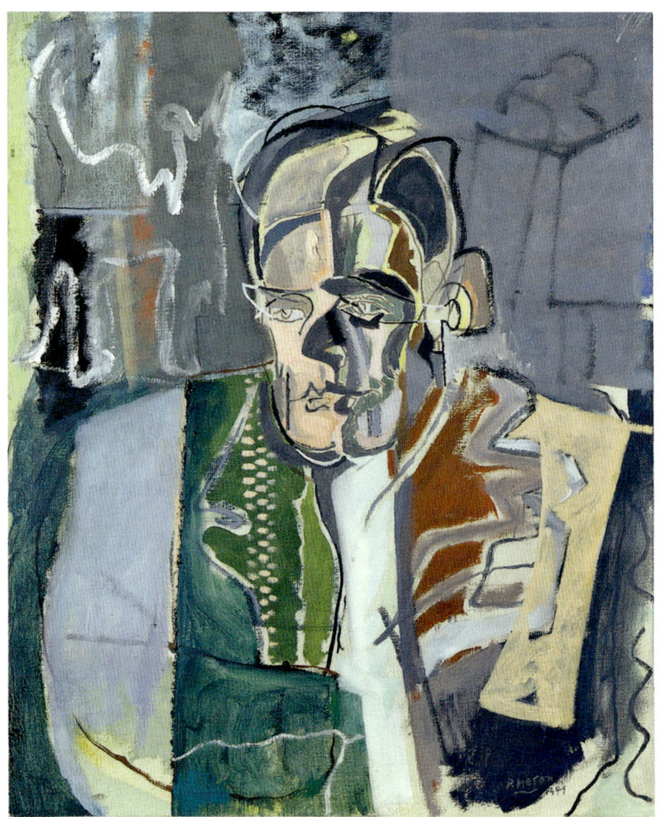

T.S. Eliot
Patrick Heron (1920–99)
Oil on canvas, 1949
762 x 629mm
NPG 4467

T.S. Eliot's poem, *The Waste Land* (1922), has been called the greatest poem of the twentieth century. In 1948 he was awarded the Nobel Prize for Literature. By 1949, when Patrick Heron painted this portrait, Eliot (1888–1965) was the most important living English-language poet and a major literary critic. After his final poetic masterpiece, *Four Quartets* (1943), the series of plays he produced from 1950 consecrated his reputation as a dramatist. From 1947 to 1950, Heron was a respected art critic, writing for the *New Statesman* and as London correspondent for the American magazine *Arts*. Before gaining recognition as one of Britain's leading abstract painters, until 1955 Heron's figurative work included portraits, still lifes and interiors with figures, which reveal the influence of Braque and Matisse. His abstracted, double-profile portrait of Eliot was based on sittings that commenced in 1947 but, eventually, was painted from memory 'very slowly, over a period of nearly three years'.

Alfred Hitchcock
Irving Penn (1917–2009)
Vintage bromide print, 1947
244 x 194mm
NPG P593

One of the twentieth-century's most celebrated and influential British film directors, Alfred Hitchcock (1899–1980) was born in Leytonstone, Essex, the son of a greengrocer. After directing the first British full-length sound film, *Blackmail* (1929), during the 1930s he went on to make several masterly films, including *The 39 Steps* and *The Lady Vanishes*, which attracted the attention of Hollywood. Moving to the United States in 1939, his films established his reputation as the 'master of suspense', a popular profile that did not detract from his innovatory methods. The photographer Irving Penn first worked for American *Vogue* in 1943. This photograph of Hitchcock dates from Penn's return to the magazine in 1947. Characteristically, Penn presented his sitter isolated against a bare studio background, enlivened only by a heap of industrial carpet. As the portrait demonstrates, this strategy of understatement focuses the presence of the subject with maximum intensity.

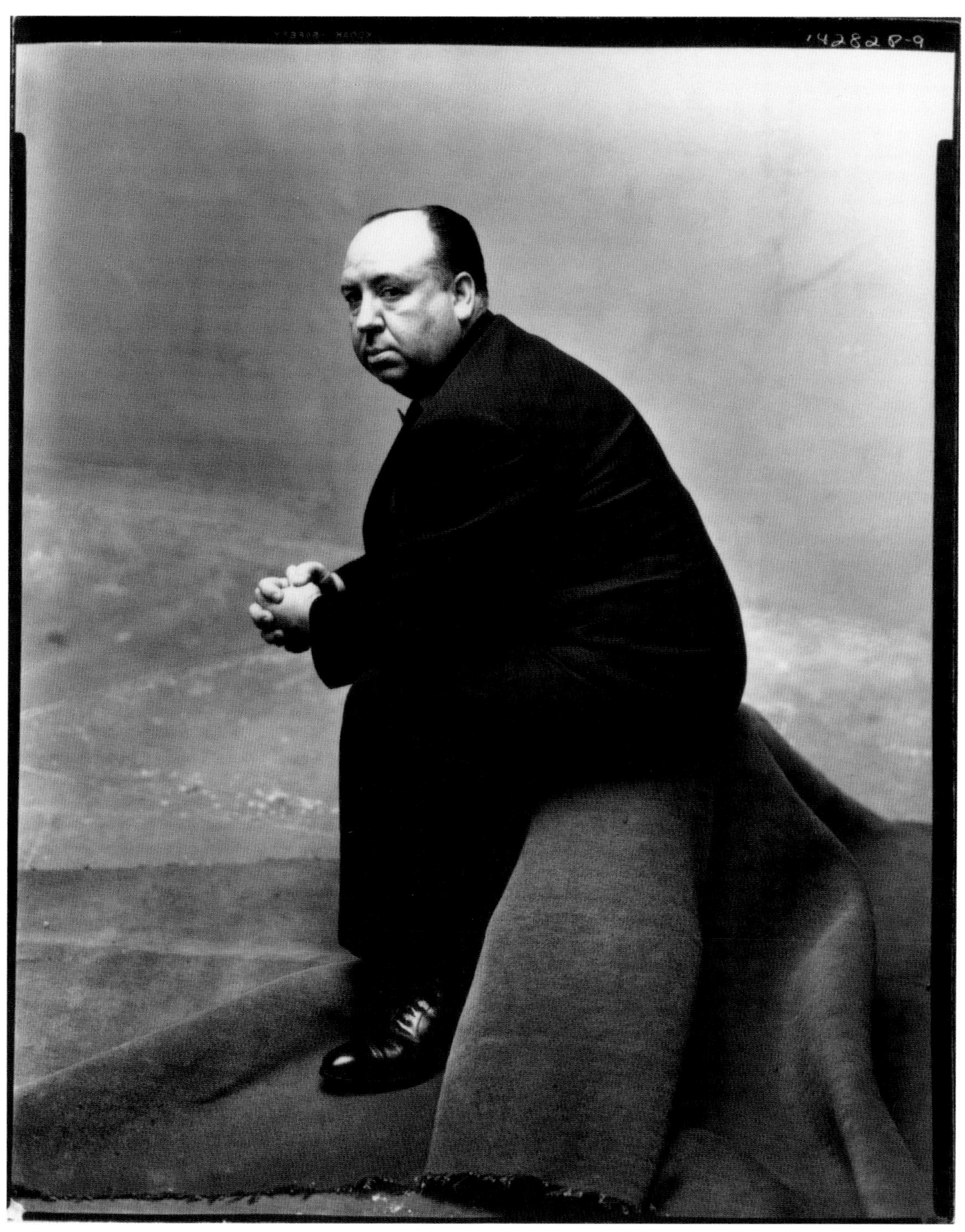

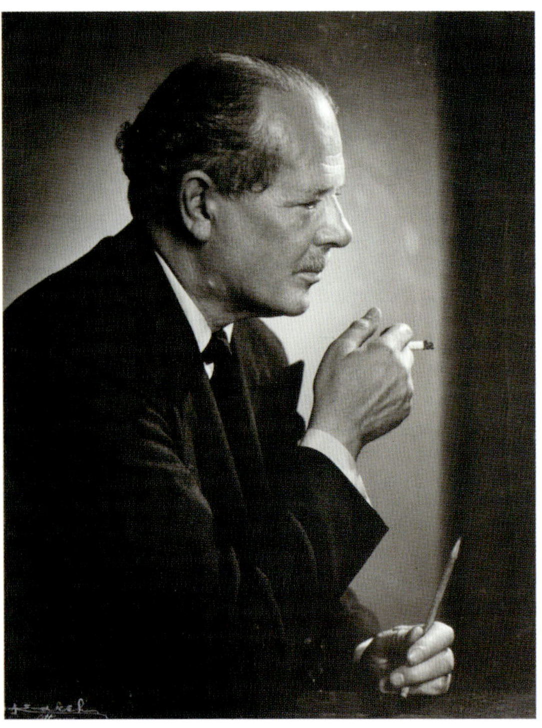

Harold Nicolson
Yousuf Karsh (1908–2002)
Bromide print, 1950
345 x 278mm
Sissinghurst Castle, Kent

Harold Nicolson's accomplishments embraced those of diplomat, politician and author. From the mid-1920s he served abroad in the Diplomatic Service, and during the Second World War he was parliamentary secretary and served as official censor in the Ministry of Information. Nicolson (1886–1968) wrote biographies of Tennyson, Byron, Swinburne, Curzon and, notably, the official life of George V. But his reputation rests chiefly on his diaries, covering the period from the 1930s to the 1950s, which provide a vital political history. At that time he was associated with the leading political and artistic figures of the day. Through his son Nigel's book, *Portrait of a Marriage*, Nicolson is also known for his then unconventional, open marriage to the writer Vita Sackville-West, with whom he created the celebrated garden at Sissinghurst Castle, Kent, which is now owned by the National Trust. This photograph forms part of the series of portraits of distinguished figures taken by Karsh from 1944 onwards.

Sir Eduardo Luigi Paolozzi
Cathleen Sabine Mann (1896–1959)
Oil on canvas, 1952
1270 x 1016mm
NPG 6005

Sculptor and printmaker Eduardo Luigi Paolozzi (1924–2005) made an important early contribution to British pop art via his celebrated 'Bunk' lecture at the Institute of Contemporary Arts in 1952, which comprised images relating to American popular culture, notably advertisements, cinema, comics and science fiction. The audience included the artist Richard Hamilton, the art critic Lawrence Alloway and others. With Paolozzi, their fascination with American urban life led to the formation of the Independent Group and a working theory of 'pop art'. Paolozzi exhibited in *This is Tomorrow* (1957), a landmark exhibition at the Whitechapel Gallery, which evoked the profusion of modern life. Paolozzi's collage-based sculpture and prints are central to pop-art iconography. Cathleen Mann's portrait depicts Paolozzi in the year of his 'Bunk' lecture. Having trained at the Slade School of Fine Art, from the mid-1920s she was a regular exhibitor at the Royal Academy and showed with the more progressive London Group.

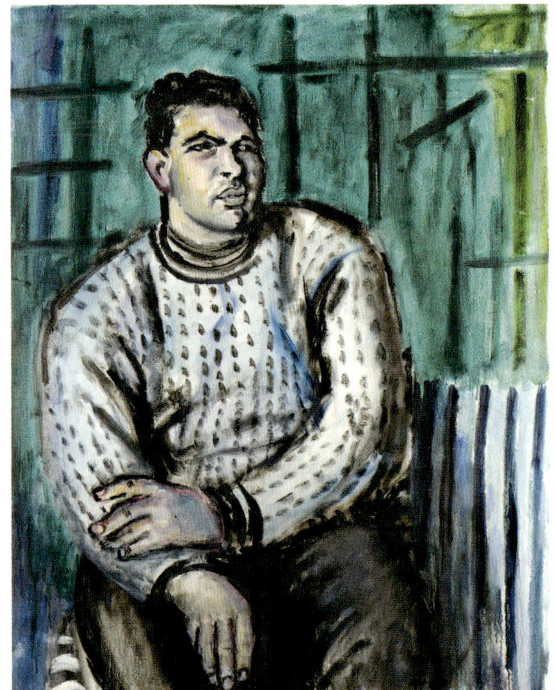

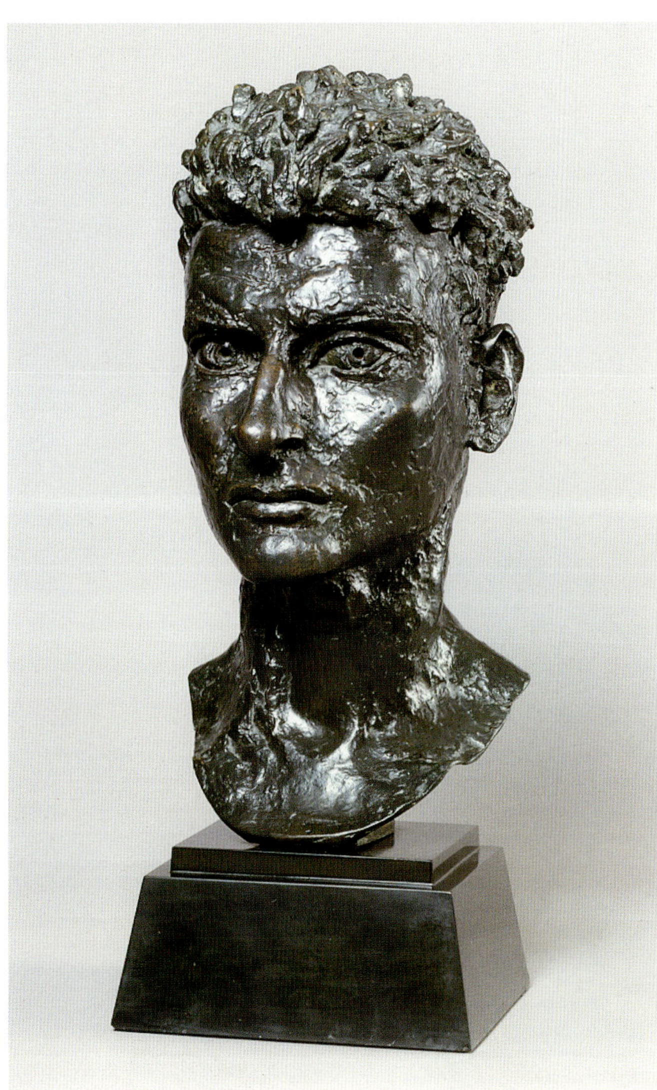

Lucian Freud
Sir Jacob Epstein (1880–1959)
Bronze head, 1949
400mm high
NPG 5199

Grandson of Sigmund Freud, the founder of
psychoanalysis, Lucian Freud (1922–2011) belonged to
a generation of young artists that achieved prominence
in Britain in the period following the Second World
War. His first solo exhibition was held in 1944, and
he showed regularly thereafter. Together with other
so-called neo-romantic artists, notably John Minton,
Keith Vaughan and John Craxton, with whom he was
linked, Freud invested figurative imagery with a
new, poetic impulse. But the heightened clarity of his
vision had a piercing, anxious quality. That tendency
towards obsessive observation gained ground in
his later portraits and nude studies, in which the
relationship between the artist and the subject has
a discomforting intensity. At the time Epstein made
this sculpture, his daughter Kitty had recently married
Freud, and the couple were living in St John's Wood,
London. Although their relationship was short-lived,
Lucian and Kitty had two daughters, whom Epstein
also portrayed.

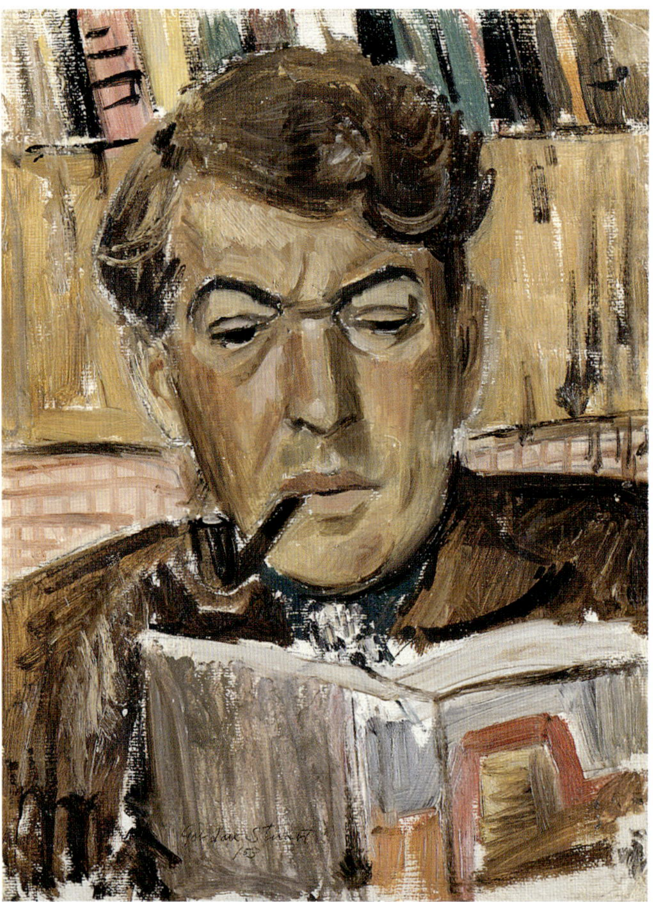

Kingsley Amis
Gordon Stuart (b.1924)
Oil on canvas board, 1953
403 x 302mm
NPG 6334

Published in 1954, Kingsley Amis's first novel, *Lucky Jim*, was an immediate success and subsequently described as the finest comic novel of its generation. It became closely associated with the 'angry young men', a term usually applied to Amis (1922–95) and other writers whose work in the 1950s was characterised as sceptical and ironic in tone and anti-establishment in outlook. Amis distanced himself from this reading of the novel. The book depicts the misfortunes of 'Jim Dixon', a lecturer at a regional university, as he attempts to progress. From 1949, Amis was an assistant lecturer in English at University College, Swansea. His subsequent novels established his reputation as an acerbic commentator on contemporary life. This portrait depicts Amis shortly before the publication of *Lucky Jim*. It was painted at Amis's house in Swansea, a sitting said by the novelist to have been 'the most frightening experience of my life'. In the same year, 1953, Stuart, who was based in Wales, painted the last portrait of the great Welsh poet Dylan Thomas.

Sir Winston Churchill
Graham Vivian Sutherland (1903–80)
Oil on canvas, 1954
345 x 311mm
NPG 5332

Defeated in the 1945 general election, Britain's greatest
wartime prime minister was returned to power in
1951, aged nearly seventy-seven. In 1953 Churchill
(1874–1965) suffered a stroke, but this was kept
secret, and he recovered. In 1954, both Houses of
Parliament commissioned a portrait from Graham
Sutherland to mark the statesman's eightieth birthday.
The commissioners specified that Churchill be depicted
in his House of Commons attire. But Churchill expected
to be shown wearing formal robes as a Knight of the
Garter. Having concealed the work in progress, when
Sutherland showed Churchill the completed portrait he
was appalled, declaring, 'It makes me look half-witted.'
When the portrait was unveiled at Westminster Hall,
Churchill pronounced it 'a remarkable example of
modern art'. The work was subsequently owned by the
sitter and, following Lady Churchill's wishes, was later
destroyed. This head study is one of a number of surviving
preparatory sketches.

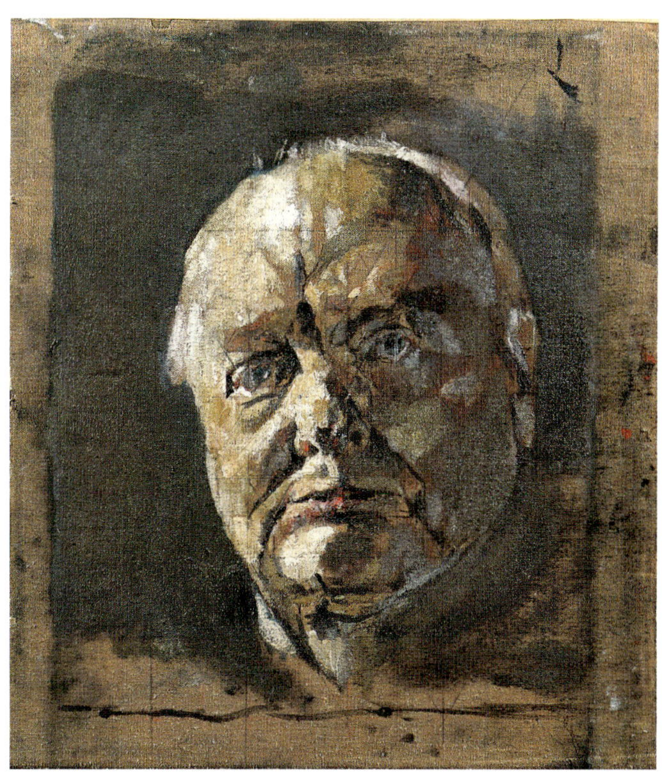

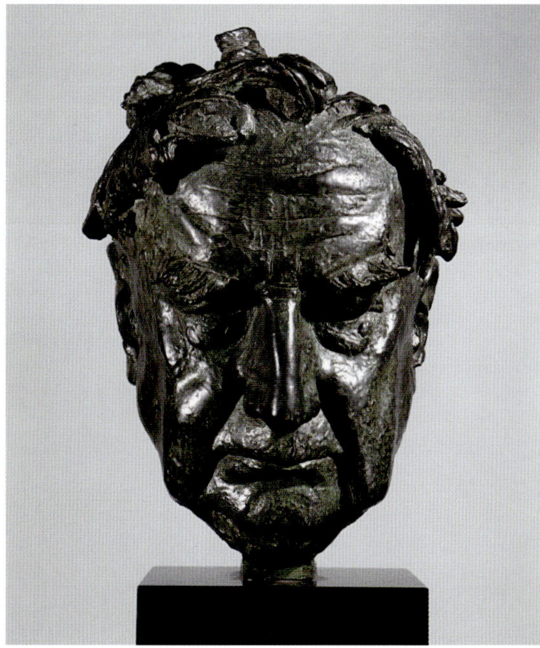

Ralph Vaughan Williams
David McFall (1919–88)
Bronze head, 1958 (1956)
318mm high
NPG 4088

A key figure in the development of British music,
Vaughan Williams (1872–1958) discovered the
English folk song in 1905, enabling the formation of
an individual style of composition that parted from
Continental models. His subsequent output was
wide-ranging, encompassing vocal and choral works,
opera, chamber pieces, film music and compositions
for orchestra, forged from both ancient and modern
elements. As a symphonist, his distinctive achievement
has few rivals among British composers. McFall's
portrait head was completed in Vaughan Williams's
study, the composer being observed over five days
while he worked at his desk. The sculptor recalled:
'He seemed lost in deep contemplation – his inward-
looking eyes were down-cast and I saw in a flash the
deep humility of the man. I worked as fast as my fingers
would go.' Vaughan Williams's widow commented:
'The likeness is extraordinary: the grave beauty of the
bronze captured the truth in strength and intimacy.'

A question of style

From the early 1960s the pace of social, political and artistic change gathered momentum. In April 1961 the Russian cosmonaut Yuri Gagarin became the first man in space. A month later President Kennedy announced the United States's decision to put an American on the moon by the end of the decade. The ensuing space race between the Soviet Union and the United States symbolised the ideological tensions between East and West that dominated the Sixties, underpinned by an ever present anxiety about nuclear war.

But alongside such tensions, a new mood of prosperity gave rise to increasing material expectations. In Britain, food rationing had ended only in 1954, and a growing affluence promised a break with the privations of the past. The mass media fuelled these changes. Television, cinema, radio, advertising and magazines swiftly communicated the latest developments in fashion, design, music, science and the arts. An atmosphere of hedonism and an appetite for greater social equality became increasingly prevalent. America achieved its epoch-making goal of a manned moon landing in 1969, but the optimism of the early 1960s was, by the end of the decade, replaced by a sense that the dream of progress had somehow slipped away. In 1973 the Arab oil-producing nations sparked an energy crisis when they embargoed shipments to the United States, Western Europe and Japan.

In Britain, strikes and growing unemployment dominated the 1970s, generating social ferment. The result was a tension between aspiration and disillusionment, in which material wealth increasingly created new hierarchies.

In the visual arts, too, traditional values were challenged. The need to reflect modern society's changing standards, and a growing emphasis on the individual's freedom of expression, led to a succession of progressive artistic movements. Pop art, op art, abstract painting and sculpture led, in the 1970s, to conceptual art, body art and land art. During this period, portraiture both reflected, and was alienated from, these developments. Portraits made in the Sixties by Sam Walsh, Larry Rivers, Howard Hodgkin, Andy Warhol and David Bailey have an affinity with popular culture. But those portraits produced in the Seventies continued earlier styles and seem adrift from more cerebral avant-garde developments. Collectively, the profusion of styles suggests a rich diversity yet, in being liberated from conventional values, a growing confusion.

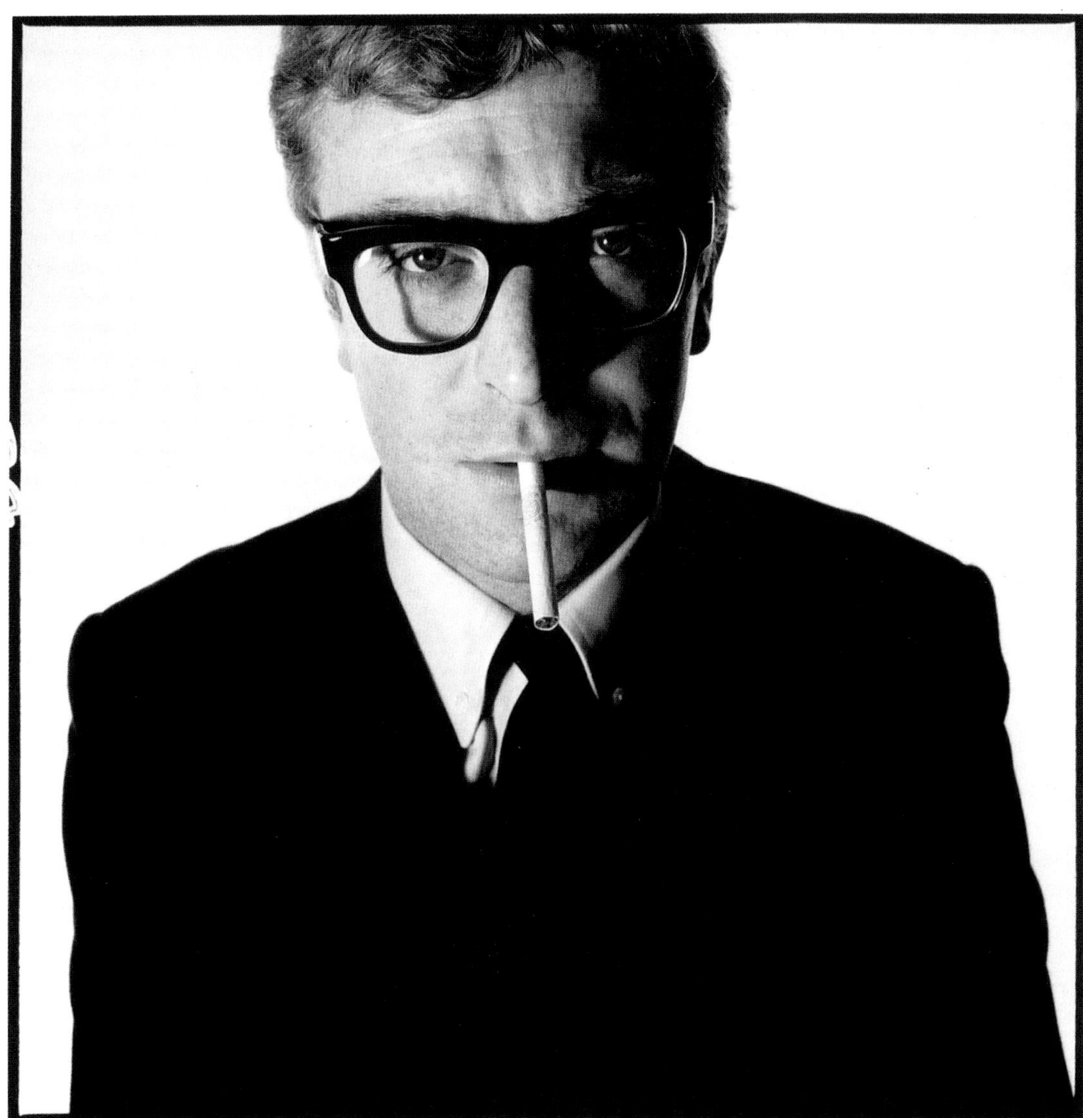

Michael Caine
David Bailey (b.1938)
Bromide print, 1965
409 x 407mm
NPG P951

Born Maurice Micklewhite, the actor Michael Caine (b.1933) shot to
fame in 1964 in the film *Zulu*. His subsequent cinematic appearances
as the spy Harry Palmer in *The Ipcress File* (1965) and in the title role
of *Alfie* (1966) established him as one of Britain's leading and most
fashionable film stars of the 1960s. As such he became associated
with the so-called Swinging London scene that developed around 1966.
This cultural phenomenon involved pop music, fashion and the media,
and was linked with celebrities such as rock musician Mick Jagger and
model Twiggy. The photographer David Bailey chronicled that scene.
Having acquired stardom in the early 1960s as a fashion photographer
for British *Vogue*, his distinctive first publication *David Bailey's Box of
Pin-Ups* (1965) comprised thirty-seven photographs of the celebrity elite
at that time. It included this portrait of Caine in role as Harry Palmer.

David Sylvester (*Mr Art*)
Larry Rivers (1923–2002)
Oil on canvas, 1962
1830 x 1370mm
NPG 6675

David Sylvester (1924–2001) dominated
British post-war modern-art criticism.
The author of numerous books,
catalogues and articles, his support
contributed to the international
reputations of Francis Bacon and Willem
de Kooning. He influenced the rise of
the international art exhibition with
seminal shows devoted to Henry Moore
(1951), Alberto Giacometti (1965) and
René Magritte (1969), among others.
His activities as a broadcaster made
him a household name in the 1950s and
1960s. Having absorbed the language
of gestural painting developed by the
Abstract Expressionists, Rivers was
one of the first artists to incorporate
imagery taken from popular culture.
That distinctive fusion of spontaneous
brushwork and recognisable subject
matter was a singular contribution to the
rise of American pop art. It forms the
basis of this portrait, which was painted
at the apex of Sylvester's public profile
in the early 1960s and at the time of
Rivers's first London exhibition.

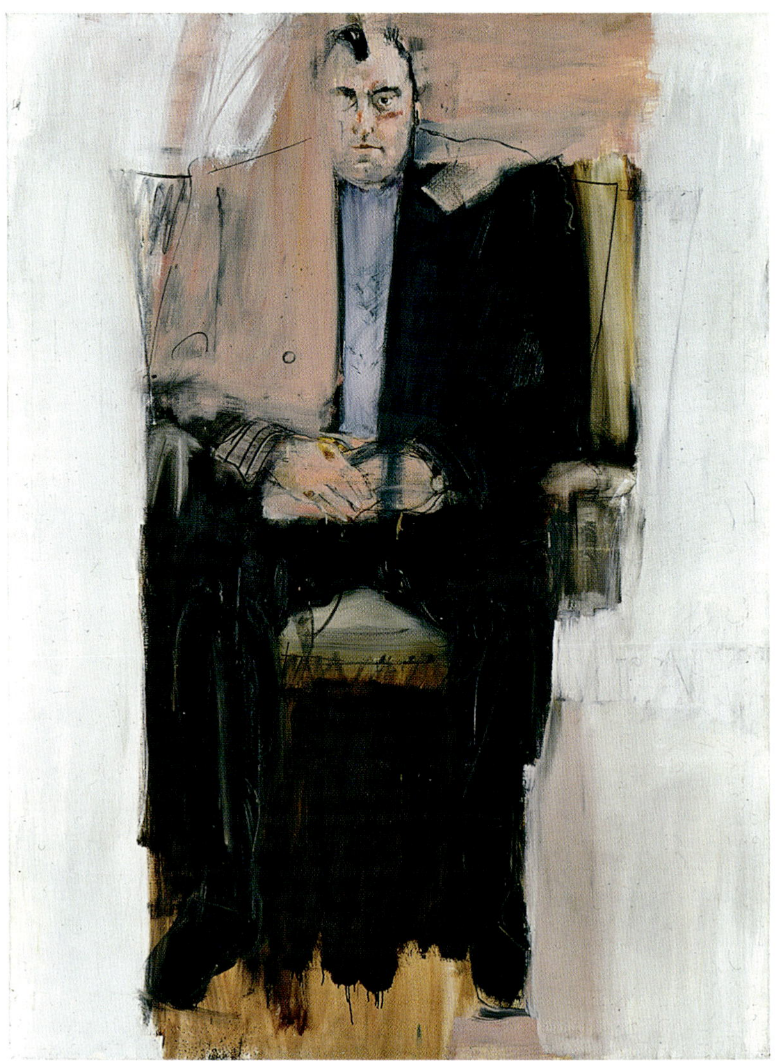

Peter Cochrane
Howard Hodgkin (b.1932)
Oil on canvas, 1962
610 x 460mm
NPG 6888

Peter Cochrane (1913–2004) was one
of the most influential art dealers of
his generation. He joined the Redfern
Gallery in 1938, then one of London's
more progressive galleries, where he
presented exhibitions of a post-war
generation of British artists including
Victor Pasmore and Patrick Heron.
After moving to Arthur Tooth & Sons
in 1950, he promoted avant-garde
European and American art. Thanks to
Cochrane, the work of Jean-Paul Riopelle,
Nicolas de Staël, Jean Dubuffet, Asger
Jorn, Sam Francis and Ellsworth Kelly
all found a British audience. During
the 1960s, his support for a younger
generation of British artists, including
Allen Jones, Peter Kinley and Howard
Hodgkin, contributed to the growing
visibility of modern art in London.
Subsequently, Cochrane continued
to influence artistic taste through
his development of an impressive
personal collection of international
twentieth-century artists. Hodgkin's
highly abstracted portrait was loosely
based on the famous Lord Kitchener
recruitment poster associated with the
First World War.

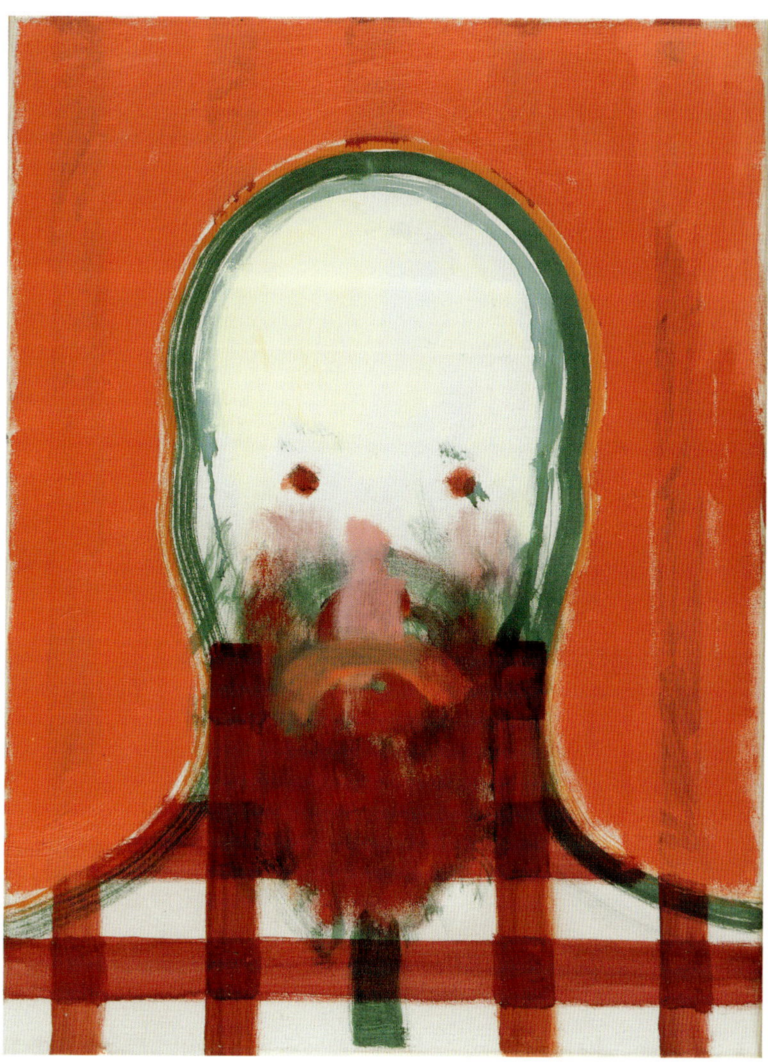

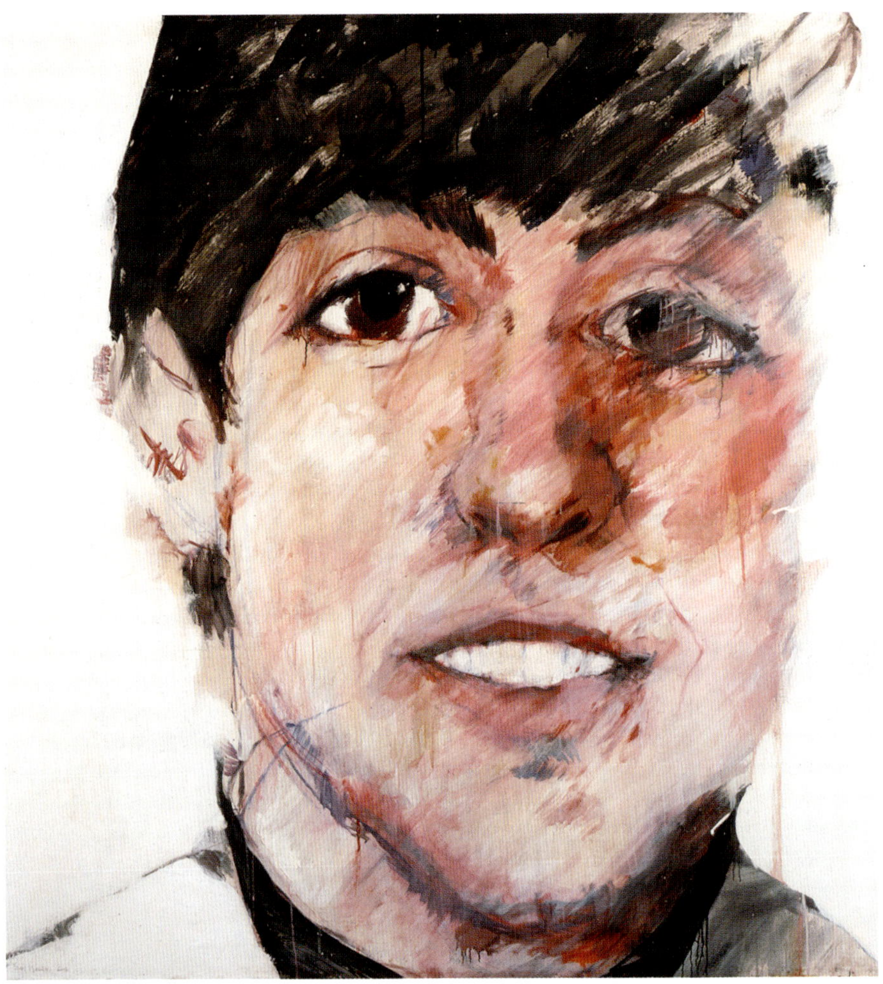

Paul McCartney *(Mike's Brother)*
Sam Walsh (1934–89)
Oil on masonite, 1964
1625 x 1550mm
NPG 6172

As a member of the pop group The Beatles, during the early 1960s Paul McCartney (b.1942) gained international fame. The Beatles first achieved mass popularity in Britain in 1962 with the success of their debut single, 'Love Me Do'. The resulting phenomenon, Beatlemania, led to acclaim in the United States and, by 1964, international recognition. Central to that success was the songwriting partnership of McCartney and John Lennon, which spanned styles and transformed popular music. Painted at the height of Beatlemania, this portrait by Walsh demonstrates the artist's distinctive combination of painterly attack and naturalism based on photography. After growing up in London, Walsh moved to Liverpool in the 1960s, attracted to the dynamic cultural scene then associated with the city. The title refers ironically to McCartney's well-known but less famous brother, who also achieved success in the 1960s as part of satirical trio The Scaffold. McCartney and Lennon's humble roots can be traced to their childhood homes 20 Forthlin Road and 'Mendips', which are now owned by the National Trust.

John Lennon
Annie Leibovitz (b.1949)
Bromide print, 1970
305 x 210mm
NPG P627

Having achieved worldwide fame with The Beatles,
whose music dominates Sixties popular culture, in 1969
John Lennon (1940–80) announced the future break-up
of the band to its other members. The release of the
group's final album, *Let It Be*, in May 1970 brought to
an end Lennon's successful songwriting partnership
with Paul McCartney. Having married the avant-garde
artist Yoko Ono in March 1969, Lennon now focused
on new, progressive musical directions with the Plastic
Ono Band, as well as releasing his highly regarded
solo album *Imagine* in 1971. At the time that he was
photographed by Leibovitz, Lennon was living in Los
Angeles. Leibovitz was then working as a photographer
for *Rolling Stone* magazine. This portrait was her first
cover for the magazine.

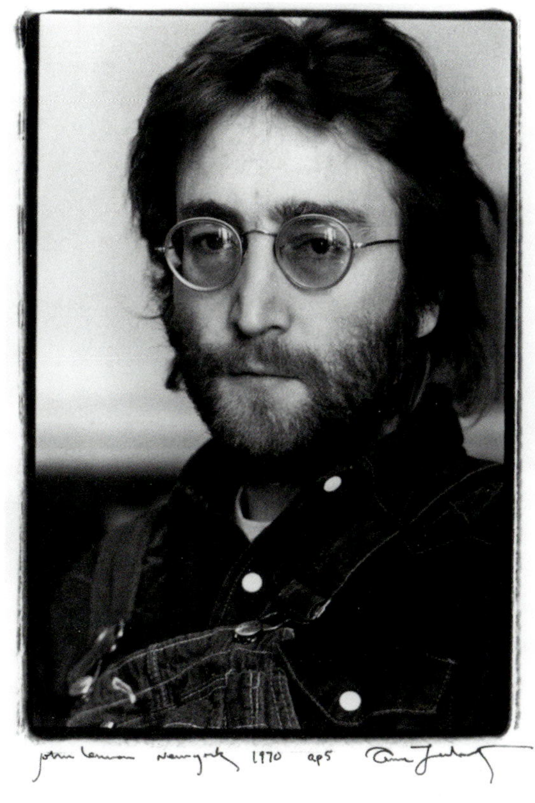

Queen Elizabeth II
Eve Arnold (1912–2012)
Cibachrome print, 1968
432 x 295mm
NPG P520

During the late 1960s, press images of Queen
Elizabeth II (b.1926) increasingly replaced the dignified
splendour of those portraits made in the previous
decade with a new, more approachable informality.
Such a change in the way the Queen was presented
and perceived reflected radical social developments.
Privileged status was increasingly at odds with a
growing egalitarianism. This photograph by Arnold, an
American photojournalist, defined the consequent shift
in the Queen's public image. In 1957, Arnold joined the
Magnum photo agency, the first woman photographer
to work there. Her remarkable, spontaneous photographs
of Marilyn Monroe, made during the filming of *The Misfits*
(1961), demonstrated a compelling intimacy. After moving
to Britain in 1961, Arnold worked for the *Sunday Times*
colour magazine. Her photograph of the Queen was
taken during a tour of Stockport. In contrast to earlier
images that emphasised the monarch's special
position, Arnold presented the Queen with a startling,
down-to-earth freshness.

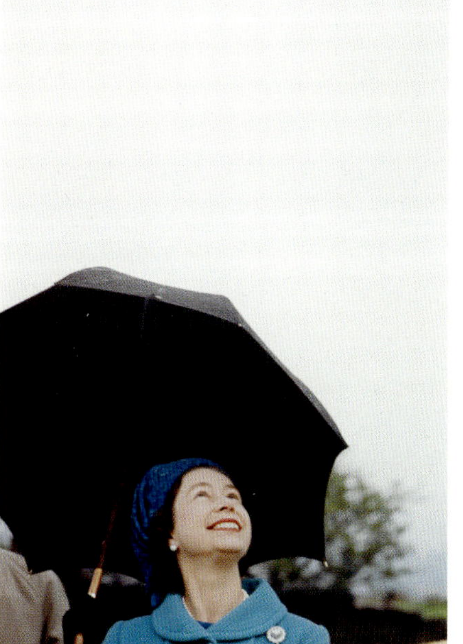

Sir Bertrand Clough Williams-Ellis
John Hedgecoe (1932–2010)
Cibachrome print, 1969
508 x 406mm
NPG P780

The architect Sir Bertrand Clough Williams-Ellis
(1883–1978) is closely associated with Portmeirion, the
Italianate village that he created on the North Wales
coast between 1925 and 1975. The spirit and atmosphere
of Portmeirion is reminiscent of the Italian village of
Portofino, not least in its distinctive sensitivity to the
relation of architecture and natural setting. Using
fragments of demolished buildings from an earlier
private estate on the site, the unique character of
Portmeirion that evolved over a fifty-year period derived
from its fusion of nostalgia and delight in decorative
detail. During its creation, these qualities set Portmeirion
apart from contemporary modernist developments, but
now seem in sympathy with the post-modernist ethos
that ensued. Hedgecoe, whose photographs appeared
in numerous magazines, depicted the architect in the
setting of his celebrated creation, capturing the dashing
dress sense for which he was known. Williams-Ellis was
appointed to transform the Stowe estate in Buckingham
into a school in 1922. The National Trust-owned gardens
are open to visitors.

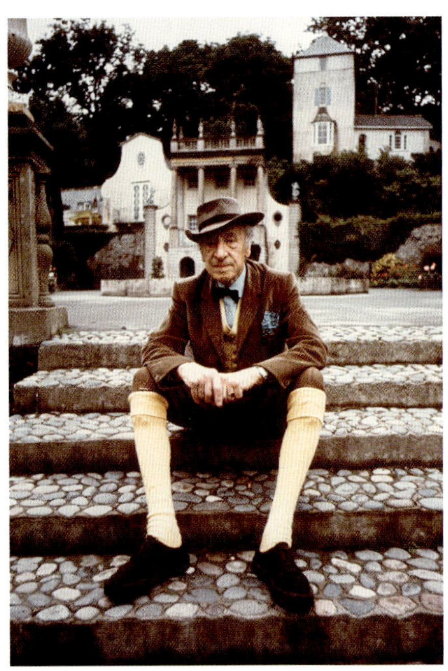

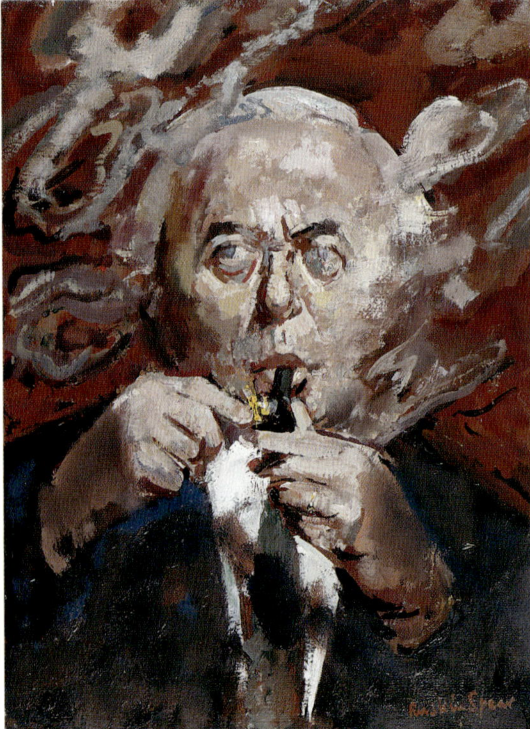

Harold Wilson
Ruskin Spear (1911–90)
Oil on canvas, exhibited 1974
511 x 381mm
NPG 5047

Until Tony Blair in the 1990s, Harold Wilson (1916–95)
was the only leader of the British Labour Party to have
led more than one Labour government. Having become
Labour leader in 1963, Wilson achieved electoral victory
in 1964 and served as British prime minister until 1970.
Despite his ambition to revitalise the economy, his
government was generally seen as a disappointment.
Devaluation in 1967, especially, was a blow to Wilson's
reputation. However, in other ways he made a
difference. Living standards improved, social services
and public welfare prospered, homosexuality was
decriminalised, and racial discrimination became a
legal offence, among other changes. Spear's portrait
dates from Wilson's return to office in 1974. The artist
was given sittings at Downing Street. Wreathed in
smoke, Wilson's ambiguous character is evoked:
both easy-going populist with trademark pipe and
elusive politician. Within two years of being re-elected,
he retired voluntarily.

David Bowie
Michael David ('Mick') Rock (b.1948)
C-type colour print, 1972
444 x 305mm
NPG P755

If The Beatles dominated popular music
during the 1960s, the most significant
and influential pop musician of the
1970s was the singer and actor David
Bowie (b.1947). Having captured public
attention in 1969 with the single
'Space Oddity', Bowie's 1972 album
*The Rise and Fall of Ziggy Stardust and the
Spiders from Mars* marked his emergence
as a cult figure. Bowie's creation in live
performance of an androgynous alter
ego, Ziggy Stardust, was one of several
roles within a career marked by stylistic
innovation and reinvention. Mick Rock's
photograph of Bowie depicts him in
role as Ziggy Stardust. It dates from
March 1972, three months before the
release of the album that transformed
his public profile, and, according to
the photographer, when the singer
was 'still essentially an "underground"
figure'. By the time the Ziggy Stardust
tour ended in July 1973, pop music had
been transformed.

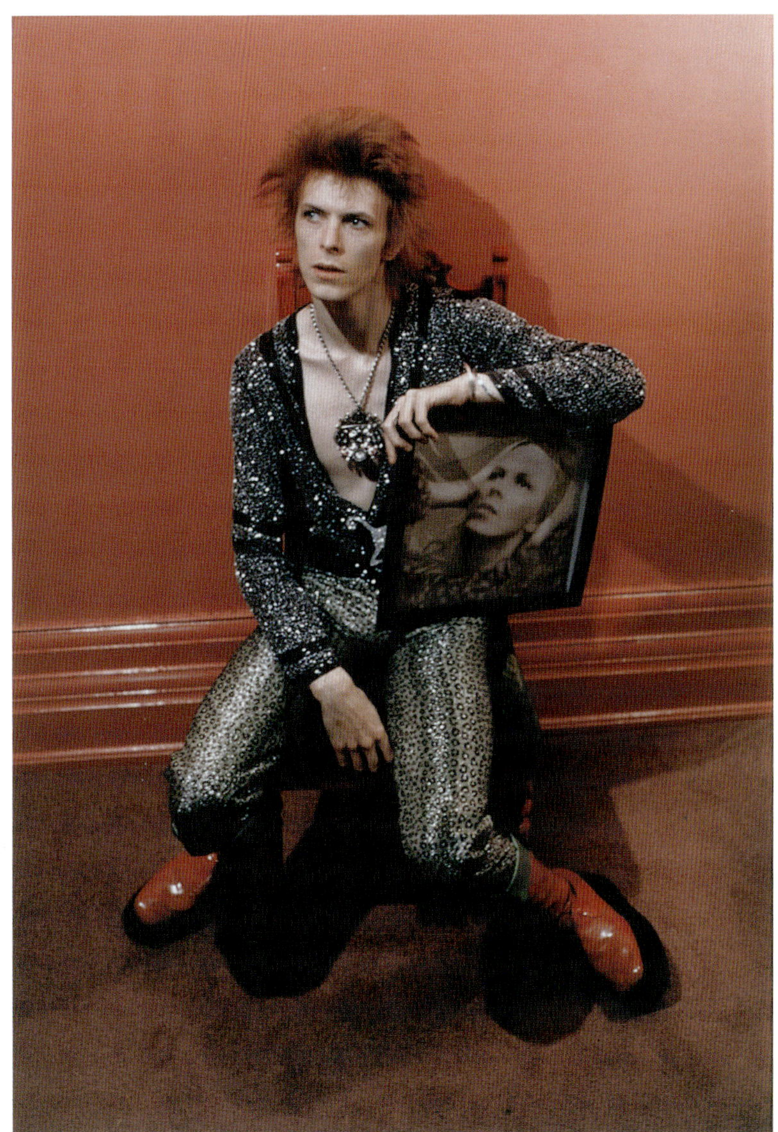

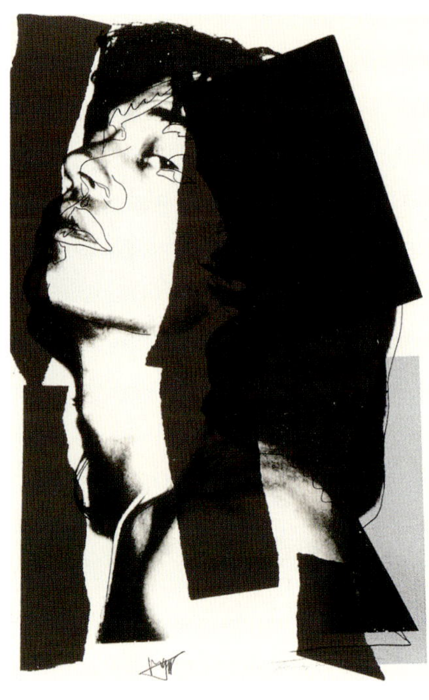

Mick Jagger
Andy Warhol (1928–87)
Silkscreen print, 1975
1115 x 735mm
NPG 6561

Singer-songwriter Mick Jagger's distinctive vocal style
and stage presence were essential to the international
popularity achieved by The Rolling Stones in the 1960s.
Formed in 1962, during that decade the rock group
achieved fifteen hit singles, including '(I Can't Get No)
Satisfaction', their first American number one in 1965.
Evoking sexual longing and frustration, the song is
inextricably linked with the changing values of an emergent
generation. In 1971, the group released *Sticky Fingers*,
which was their first album to make number one on both
sides of the Atlantic and featured a cover by Andy Warhol.
This portrait of Jagger (b.1943) by Warhol dates from the
group's Tour of the Americas '75, which opened in New
York. During the 1970s, Warhol's longstanding fascination
with fame focused increasingly on society portraits
depicting the wealthy and the famous. The Jagger image
belongs to a set of ten, in which, characteristically, Warhol
exposed the artifice inherent in creating a modern 'icon'.

Graham Sutherland
Self-portrait
Oil on canvas, 1977
527 x 502mm
NPG 5338

Portraiture was an integral, if not substantial aspect
of Sutherland's oeuvre. Initially a printmaker, in 1934
Sutherland (1903–80) discovered the landscape of
Pembrokeshire that subsequently provided inspiration
for paintings that explored the anthropomorphic
character of natural forms. From the early 1940s,
his art moved towards figure painting and eventually
began to embrace portraiture, although the number of
commissions he accepted was limited. Notable sitters
included Somerset Maugham, Lord Beaverbrook and
Sir Winston Churchill. Sutherland's method involved
making drawings and sometimes oil sketches from
life. On occasion, photographs would be taken as
supporting material. He would then make a final
portrait in the absence of the sitter, based on the
studies. Throughout the sittings, the artist would await
an expression or pose that appeared characteristic,
his aim to convey 'psychological truth'. This self-
portrait was painted for an exhibition of Sutherland's
portraits at the National Portrait Gallery in 1977.

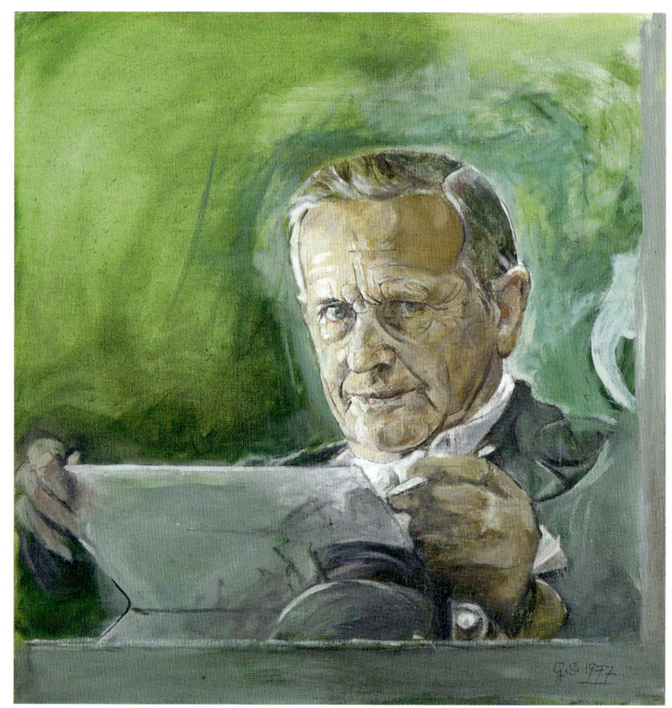

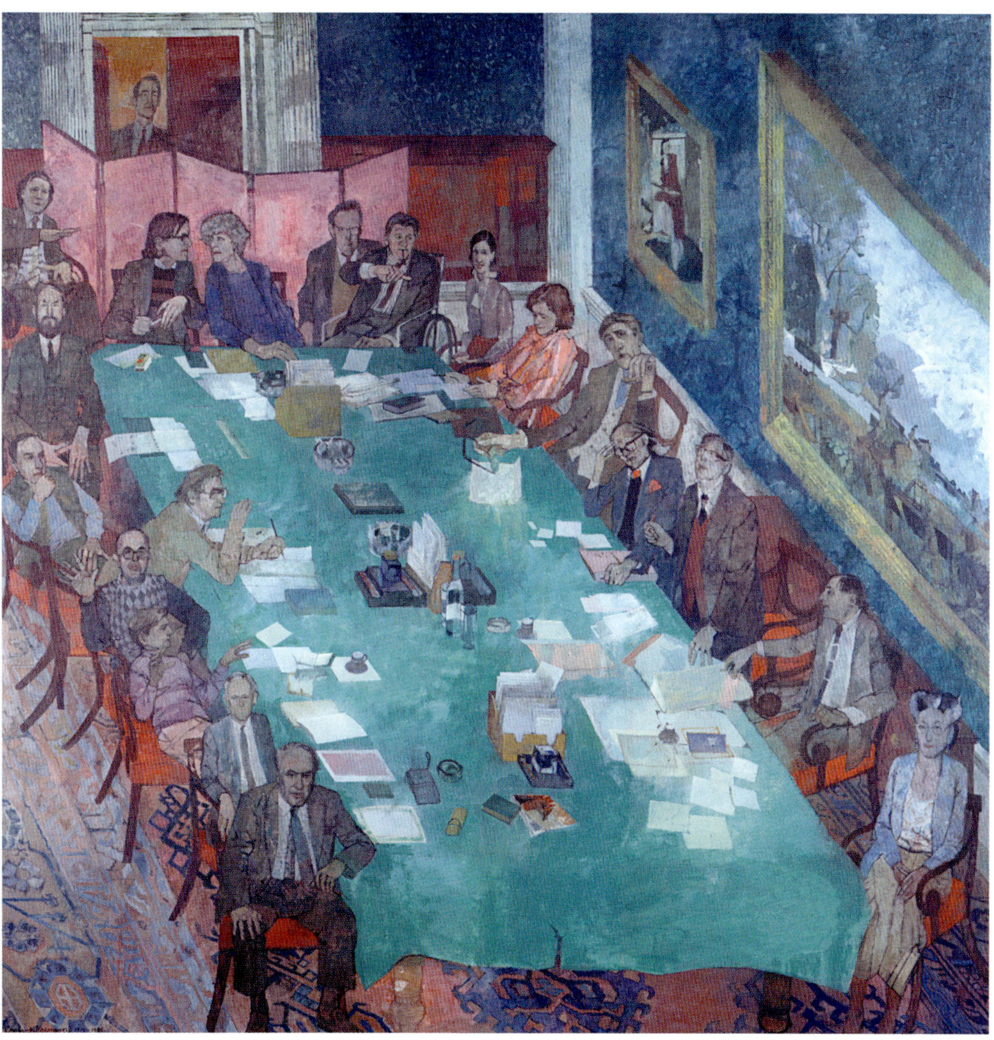

The Meeting, Royal Academy of Arts
Leonard Rosoman (1913–2012)
Acrylic on canvas, 1979–84
1524 x 1524mm
NPG 5740

Until the mid-1960s, the Royal Academy (RA) was perceived as a bastion of tradition, standing in defiance of modern art. However, during Charles Wheeler's presidency (1956–66), a rapprochement was set in train. In his penultimate year, the *Daily Mail* noted that 'the RA stops snubbing the moderns'. Under subsequent presidents, the RA's admission of more avant-garde artists, and a progressive exhibition programme, demonstrated the changed outlook. Leonard Rosoman, who became a Royal Academician in 1969 and was then teaching at the Royal College of Art, was instrumental in these developments. In this group portrait he depicted his fellow RA members – artists and employees – and recorded: 'Sitting at the Council table during a meeting, I found the movements flickering in and around the 20 figures absorbing, and started to make notes and drawings instead of the usual doodles.' This was the genesis of *The Meeting*, which took five years to complete.

Towards a new millennium

The final two decades of the twentieth century saw the gradual transition from global economic recession at the beginning of the 1980s to increasing prosperity during the 1990s. In most Western countries economic growth was matched by falling unemployment, marking a period of sustained affluence. During the same time-span the revolution in communication that defines the century as a whole came of age. Following the appearance of commercially available home computers in the mid-1980s, in 1989 Sir Tim Berners-Lee invented the World Wide Web. The Internet revolution that ensued made the electronic exchange of information available to the public, transforming the way people conducted business, their relationship with society and their personal lives.

In Britain, an adherence to traditional values was sustained alongside more progressive social and artistic forces. Bryan Organ's portrait of Diana, Princess of Wales, painted in 1981, depicts an individual who captured the imagination and attention of a generation. For many, her marriage to Prince Charles, and her subsequent presence in the public eye, reinvigorated the concept of royalty, infusing it with an unfamiliar degree of celebrity. For others, her ensuing marital rift, and the cult of personality that surrounded Diana, exposed the irrelevance of monarchy within a modern, egalitarian society. The ninth decade of the twentieth century was also dominated in Britain by its first woman prime minister, Margaret Thatcher, whose portrait by Rodrigo Moynihan shows her, following her re-election to a second term of office in 1983. Thatcher oversaw a turbulent period that involved riots, war in the Falklands, conflict in Northern Ireland and confrontation with the trade unions.

The portraits that define the 1980s and 1990s – when modernism gave way to the so-called post-modern period – extended the ever increasing stylistic diversity that had commenced in the 1960s. Alongside the expressive figuration of Lucian Freud's 1989 portrait of Lord Rothschild, there is the graphic impersonality of Andy Warhol's portraits of the Queen. In the 1990s, the acerbic, confrontational quality of Sarah Lucas's self-portrait defines the YBAs or Young British Artists, a group that embraced irony, shock tactics and insouciance. Nevertheless, the growing, media-generated infatuation with celebrity that gained ground also prized glamour, as Mario Testino's 1996 portrait of the supermodel Kate Moss demonstrates. Absorbing these contrasts, as the twentieth century drew to a close, portraiture reclaimed centre stage, holding a mirror to those responsible for a changing world and its future.

Diana, Princess of Wales
Bryan Organ (b.1935)
Acrylic on canvas, 1981
1778 x 1270mm
NPG 5408

The youngest daughter of the 8th Earl
Spencer, Lady Diana Spencer was
first connected with Prince Charles,
heir to the British throne, in 1980.
Their engagement was announced in
February 1981, and the subsequent
wedding at Westminster Abbey on
29 July 1981 was broadcast live to
some 750 million people in seventy-four
countries. From the outset, Princess
Diana (1961–97) attracted enormous
popularity, and her celebrity status,
nurtured by high-profile visibility in the
media, reinvigorated public interest in
the British monarchy. However, growing
rumours about the disintegration of
Charles and Diana's relationship led
to divided loyalties for the public.
Separated in 1992 and divorced in 1996,
Diana was killed in a car crash in Paris
in 1997. Commissioned by the National
Portrait Gallery in 1981, Bryan Organ had
six sittings and completed the portrait
in seven weeks, working from sketches
and photographs. It was unveiled at
the Gallery on 23 July 1981, six days
before the wedding.

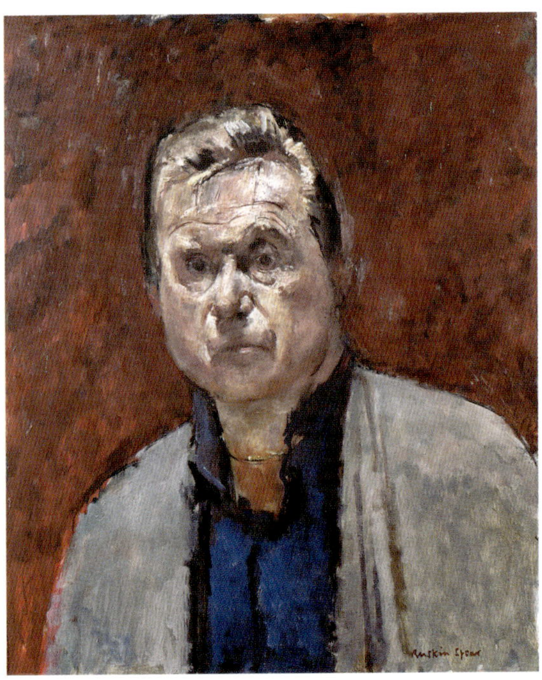

Francis Bacon
Ruskin Spear (1911–90)
Oil on board, 1984
762 x 632mm
NPG 5818

Described by Margaret Thatcher as 'the man who
paints those dreadful pictures', Francis Bacon
(1909–92) was regarded by many as the greatest
living British artist. However, his uncompromising
vision of the human condition was controversial. First
exhibited in 1945, his triptych, *Three Studies for Figures
at the Base of a Crucifixion*, established his reputation.
But its depiction of grotesque, semi-human figures
announced an outlook rooted in violence to the image,
characterised by deformation and expressive distortion.
The international recognition he secured linked him
with existentialist ideas according to which, devoid of
divine guidance, man occupies a self-made hell. Bacon
himself regarded his imagery as a way of assaulting the
viewer's nervous system in order to intensify its impact,
observing that the artist 'must really deepen the game'.
By 1984, when Spear painted Bacon, the sitter had held
major exhibitions worldwide, his place in the annals of
twentieth-century art secure.

Margaret Thatcher, Baroness Thatcher
Rodrigo Moynihan (1910–90)
Oil on canvas, 1983–5
1265 x 1015mm
NPG 5728

Elected British prime minister in 1979, Margaret Thatcher
(b.1925) was the first woman to hold this office.
Nicknamed 'the Iron Lady', she was re-elected in 1983
and 1987, this period of continuous Conservative policy
leading to the 1980s being identified with Thatcherism.
Under Thatcher British economic and foreign policy
shifted to the right. In 1982 she attracted public support
when the Falkland Islands were invaded by the Argentine
junta, and she successfully despatched a Task Force to
repel the invasion. In 1984, she defeated a longstanding
strike by the miners' union. However, a proposed tax for
local government, the 'poll tax', was deeply unpopular,
and declining support within her own party resulted in her
resignation in 1990. Painted at 10 Downing Street over
the course of two years, Rodrigo Moynihan's portrait was
initially controversial. The sitter objected to the artist's
treatment of her eyes, but later approved his corrections.

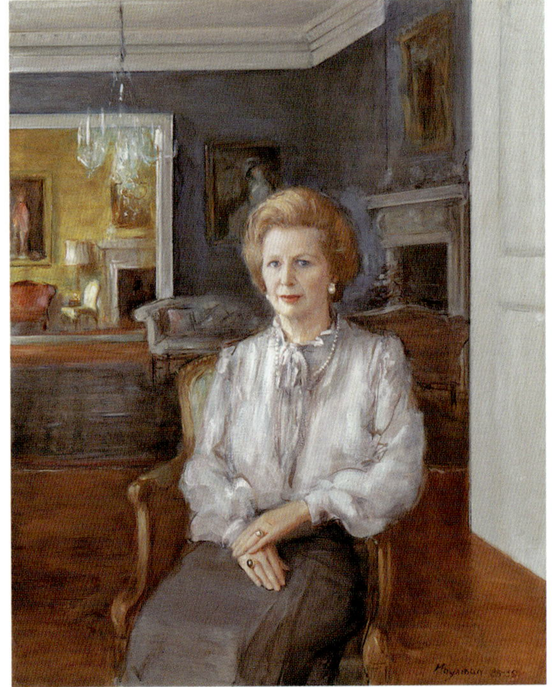

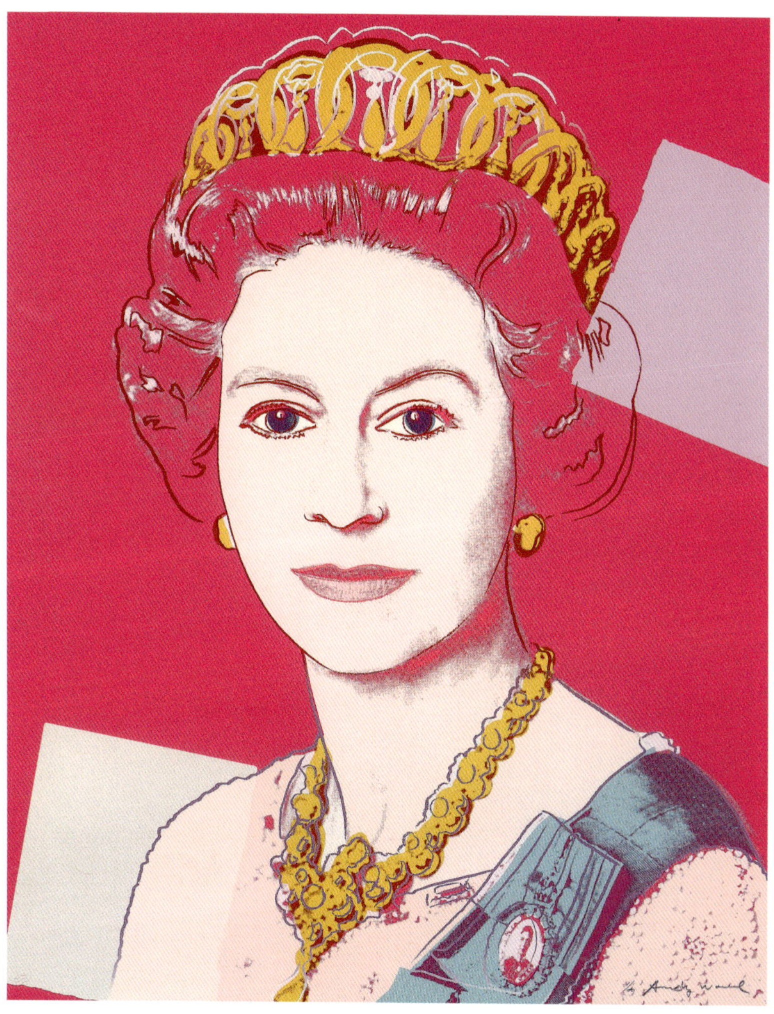

Queen Elizabeth II
Andy Warhol (1928–87)
Silkscreen print, 1985
1000 x 800mm
NPG 5882(4)

A pioneer of pop art in America in the early 1960s, Andy Warhol engaged with an emergent consumer culture characterised by mass production and the mass media. Images appropriated from popular culture, often repeated in series to simulate mechanical reproduction, dominate his iconography. With portraiture at the centre of his prolific output, Warhol depicted leading celebrities of the time, including Marilyn Monroe, Elvis Presley and Elizabeth Taylor. By his own admission, he was fascinated by fame. With his portraits of Elizabeth II (b.1926), he took one of the world's most famous individuals, and, in common with his other portraits, dissected the process by which a real person acquires a public image and becomes an 'icon'. Basing the portraits on an original photograph, Warhol abstracted the features, embellishing the Queen's face with line, heightened colour and non-descriptive shapes. The result is a tension between the person depicted and a fabricated, mask-like surface, evoking fame's artificial nature.

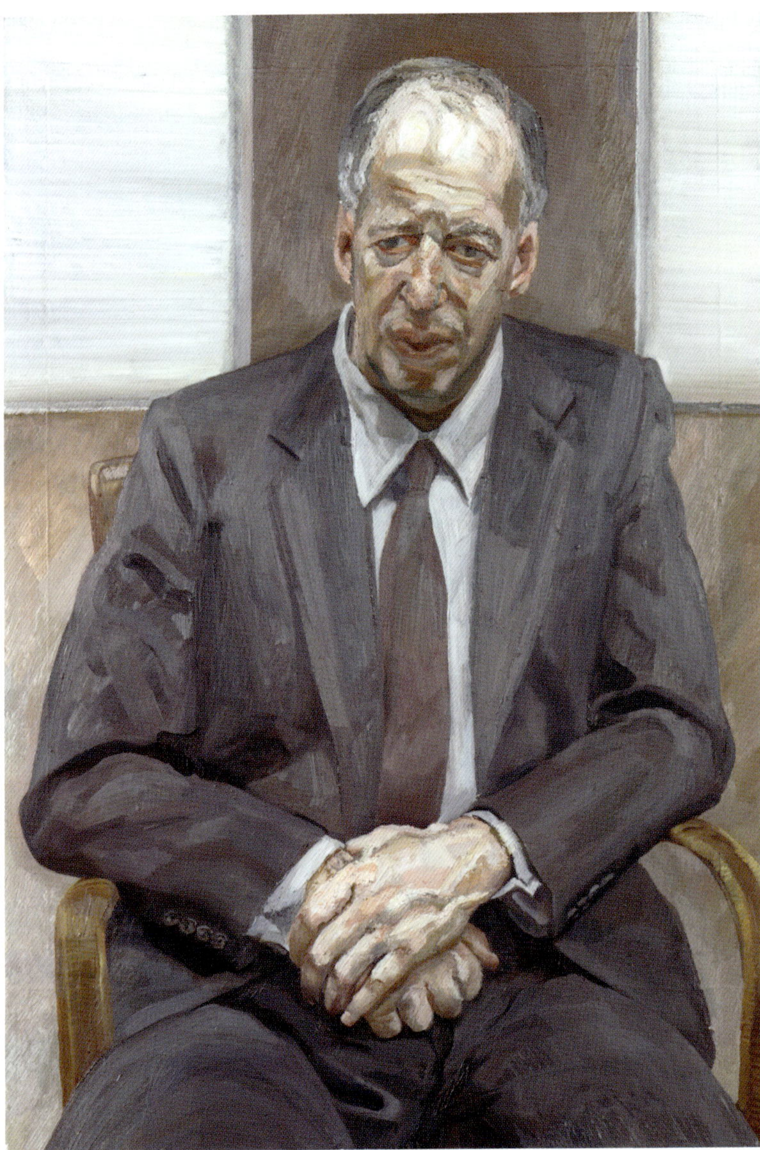

Jacob Rothschild (*Man in a Chair*)
Lucian Freud (1922–2011)
Oil on canvas, 1989
1143 x 797mm
NPG L201

Jacob Rothschild (b.1936) is a prominent banker and patron of the arts. He is descended from the Rothschild dynasty, a family of German–Jewish origin responsible for establishing an empire of banks and finance houses in the eighteenth century. At its height, the family amassed the largest fortune in history. Jacob Rothschild resigned from the family bank, N.M. Rothschild & Sons, in 1980. Among numerous chairmanships, he now controls RIT Capital Partners, one of the largest investment trusts on the London Stock Exchange. A distinguished philanthropist for the arts in Britain, he was chairman of trustees at the National Gallery and, among other associations, is a major benefactor of Waddesdon Manor, one of the National Trust's major properties. As the title of this painting suggests, Freud's portrait is deliberately understated, with no intimation of the sitter's background or position. Characteristically, its intense focus is on a human presence.

Sir Tim Berners-Lee
Fergus Greer
Bromide fibre print, 2000
375 x 380mm
NPG x88859

As the inventor of the World Wide Web, Sir Tim
Berners-Lee (b.1955) has profoundly influenced the
modern world. Extending those radical developments
in communication that define the twentieth century,
his proposal in 1989 enabled individuals to combine
their knowledge in an electronic web of hypertext
documents. The first server went online on Christmas
Day 1990, heralding the subsequent global spread
and use of Web technology. In 1999, *Time* magazine
described him as one of the 100 greatest minds of the
century. Just over twenty years earlier, in 1976, Berners-
Lee had built his first computer, using a soldering
iron, an old television and rudimentary processing
equipment. Berners-Lee is now director of the World
Wide Web Consortium. Founded in 1994, its aim is to
develop the Web's potential in the twenty-first century.
The work of the portrait photographer Fergus Greer
is characterised by intensive preparatory research and
actively involves the sitter as a participant.

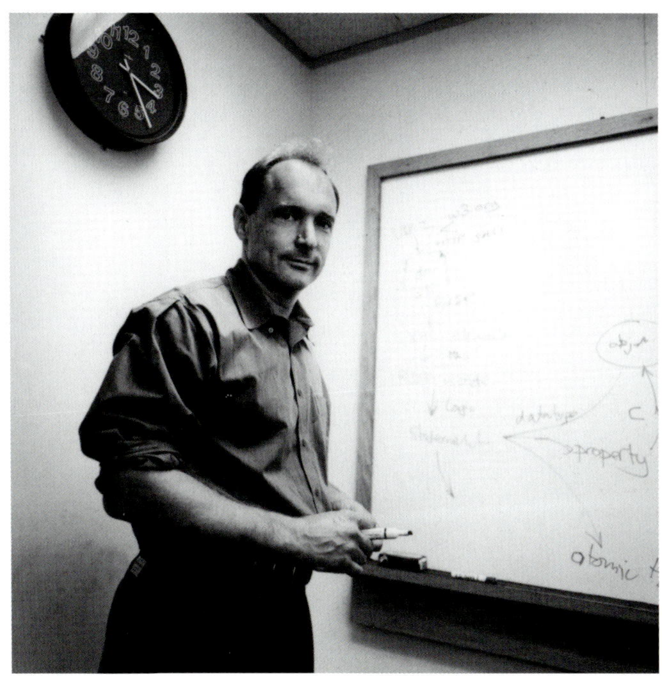

Sir Ernst Gombrich
R.B. Kitaj (1932–2007)
Pastel and charcoal, 1986
676 x 578mm
NPG 5892

E.H. Gombrich's *The Story of Art* (1950) was among the
most widely read and influential books on art history
in the second half of the twentieth century. With his
many other important publications, including *Art and
Illusion* (1960), *Norm and Form* (1966) and *The Sense
of Order* (1979), it established Gombrich (1909–2001)
as one of the leading art historians of his generation.
Whether writing about primitive, classical, medieval or
renaissance art, Gombrich's approach was rooted in
the psychology of perception and the history of ideas.
Born and educated in Vienna, Gombrich settled in
England in 1936. After joining the Warburg Institute
in the same year, he was director and professor of the
History of the Classical Tradition there from 1959 to
1976. Associated with the early formation of pop art,
Kitaj later developed a distinctive style of figurative
art closely connected with his Jewish background.
Scrupulous observer that he was, Gombrich disliked
Kitaj's portrait, doubting its veracity as a likeness.

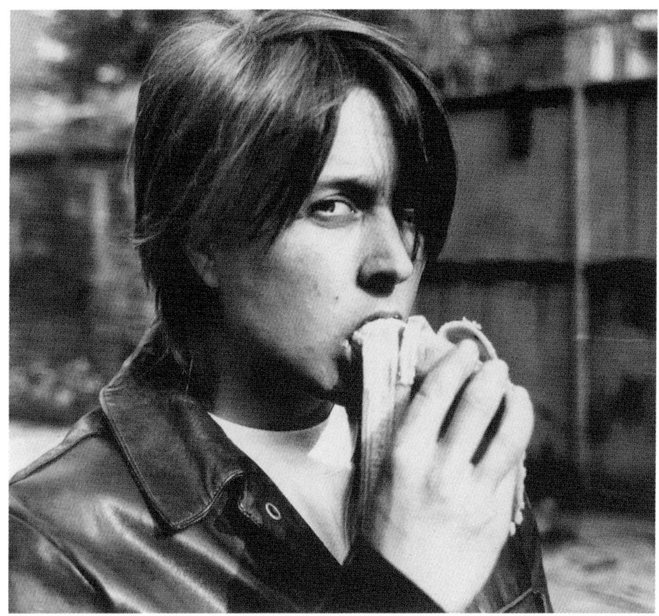

Sarah Lucas *(Eating a Banana)*
Self-portrait
Iris print, 1990
540 x 598mm
NPG P884(1)

Sarah Lucas (b.1962) was one of the original sixteen artists who exhibited in *Freeze* in 1988. Organised by Damien Hirst, the exhibition was associated with the emergence of the Young British Artists (YBAs), a generation that came to define British art in the 1990s. Among the YBAs, Lucas's work is distinctive. Involving photography and also sculpture and installations using found objects, her principal themes are gender, sex and, as in this portrait, personal identity. Returning to herself as subject in a series of photographic self-portraits, Lucas's work connects with the fascination with celebrity, individualism and 'attitude' said to characterise society since the 1980s. As this portrait demonstrates, Lucas deliberately presents herself in a way that appears confrontational yet apparently vacuous. The implication is that any banal action – whether eating a banana or, as in another self-portrait, sitting on a toilet – is sufficient in an image-obsessed age.

Kate Moss
Mario Testino (b.1954)
Durst and Lambda bromide print, 1996
515 x 408mm
NPG P1020

One of the world's highest-earning fashion models, Kate Moss (b.1974) both dominated and changed the style of modelling during the 1990s, creating a fusion of fashion and celebrity. Her career commenced in 1988 at the age of fourteen, when, at JFK airport in New York, she attracted the attention of Sarah Doukas, the founder of Storm model agency. Moss subsequently appeared in the *Face* and *Vogue*. At eighteen, she featured in a highly publicised campaign for underwear designed by Calvin Klein. Pioneering the 'waif' look, her diminutive figure contrasted with that of other, curvaceous models and sparked controversy about eating disorders. Her ubiquity on magazine covers, and association with numerous major international designers and photographers, conferred an iconic profile. Mario Testino, whose fashion photography is associated with Gucci, Versace, Gap and Burberry, took this photograph in Los Angeles in 1996. It appeared in the American edition of *Harper's Bazaar*.

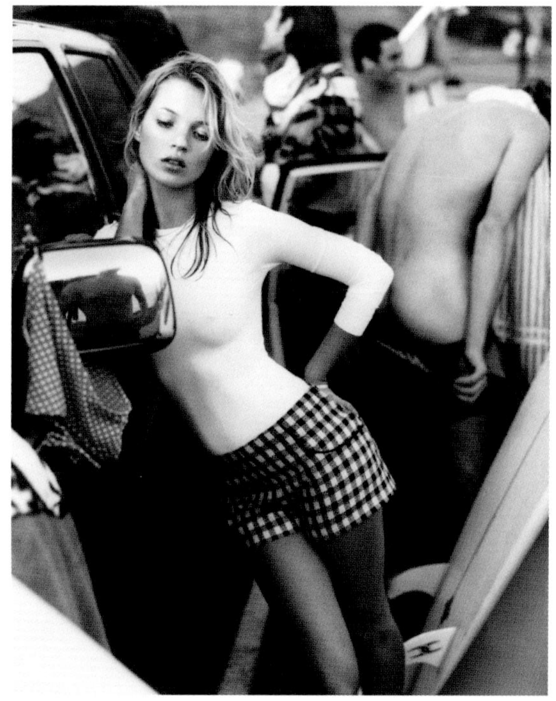

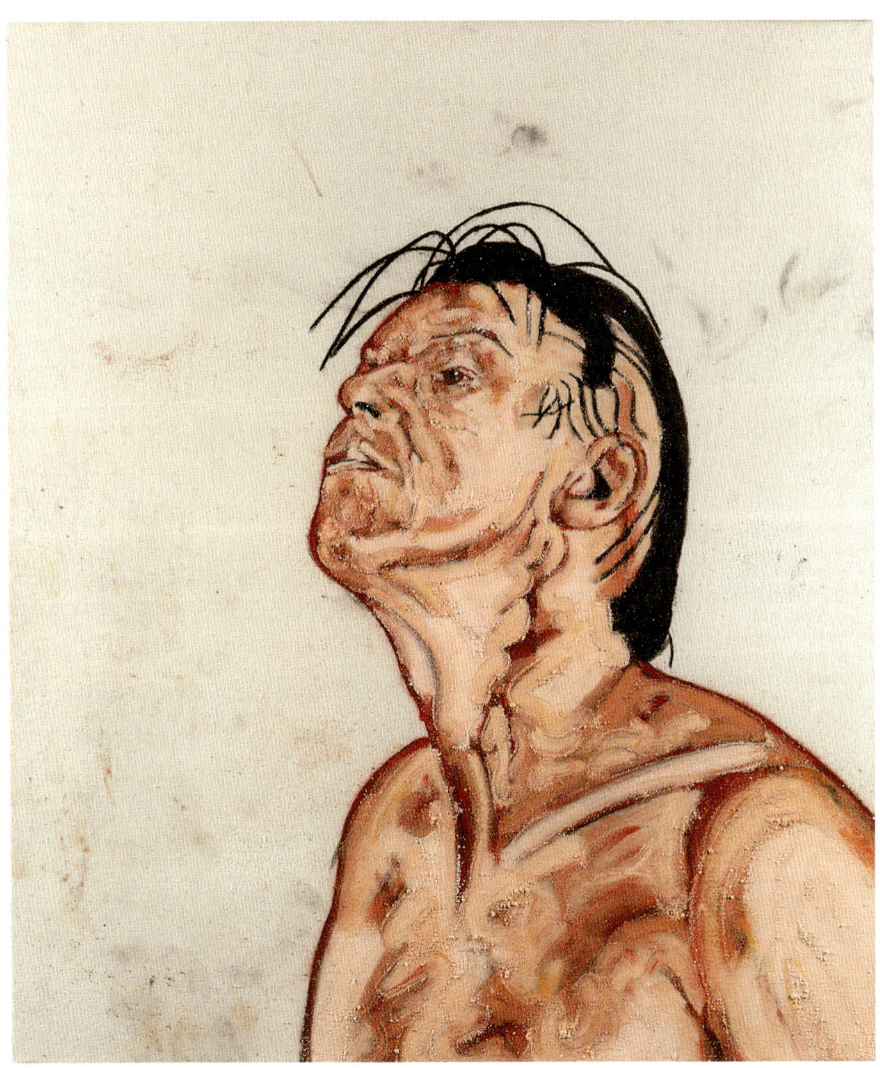

Tony Bevan
Self-portrait
Oil and pigment on canvas, 1992
878 x 757mm
NPG 6818

Since the early 1980s, when Tony Bevan (b.1951) first attracted attention, the central theme of his work has been the depiction of the human figure. Although Bevan's imagery encompasses other subjects, including corridors and abandoned buildings, his engagement with representing individuals and with parts of the body, especially the head and neck, is a defining characteristic of his art. Within that approach, self-portraiture has been a major tributary of images. Initially covert, Bevan's use of his own features as subject became explicit in 1987. Using a mirror or photographs, the artist's own appearance is recorded in drawings, which, in being progressively abstracted, then form the basis of paintings. As this portrait from 1992 demonstrates, the achievement of an accurate likeness is not a primary aim. Rather, his own presence provides a starting point for imaginative development, the act of portrayal leading instead to an image that has an autonomous, expressive character.

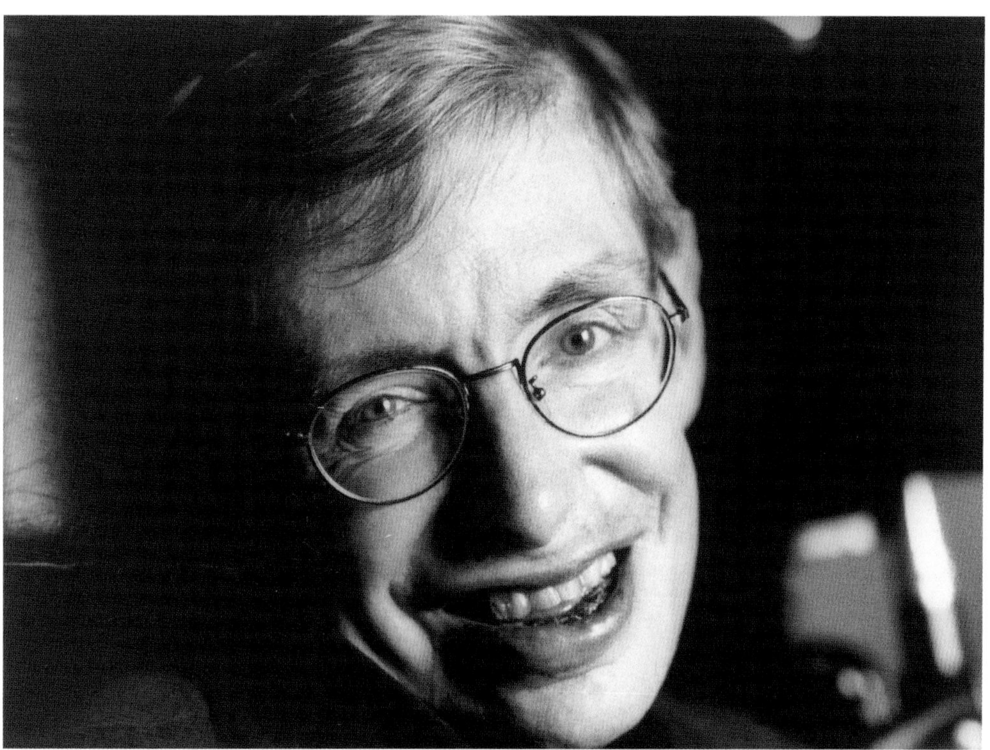

Stephen Hawking
Jane Bown (b.1925)
Bromide print, 1999
256 x 354mm
NPG P758(4)

Among his many distinguished publications,
Stephen Hawking's *A Brief History of Time* was
an unanticipated success and brought its author
widespread recognition. Published in 1988, this
popular study of cosmology broke best-seller records
and, when issued in paperback, reached number one in
the best-sellers list in three days. The book drew upon
Hawking's work on general relativity, which used new
mathematical techniques to develop innovatory ideas
within cosmology. Hawking (b.1942) held the position
(1979–2009) of Lucasian Professor of Mathematics at
Cambridge University, a post previously occupied by
Sir Isaac Newton. By the mid-1980s, the motor neurone
disease that has afflicted Hawking since the early
1960s had become severely disabling, necessitating
the use of a computer system to provide an electronic
voice. Jane Bown's portrait of Hawking exemplifies
the photographer's distinctive, informally posed
approach, employing natural light and frequently
relying on one shot.

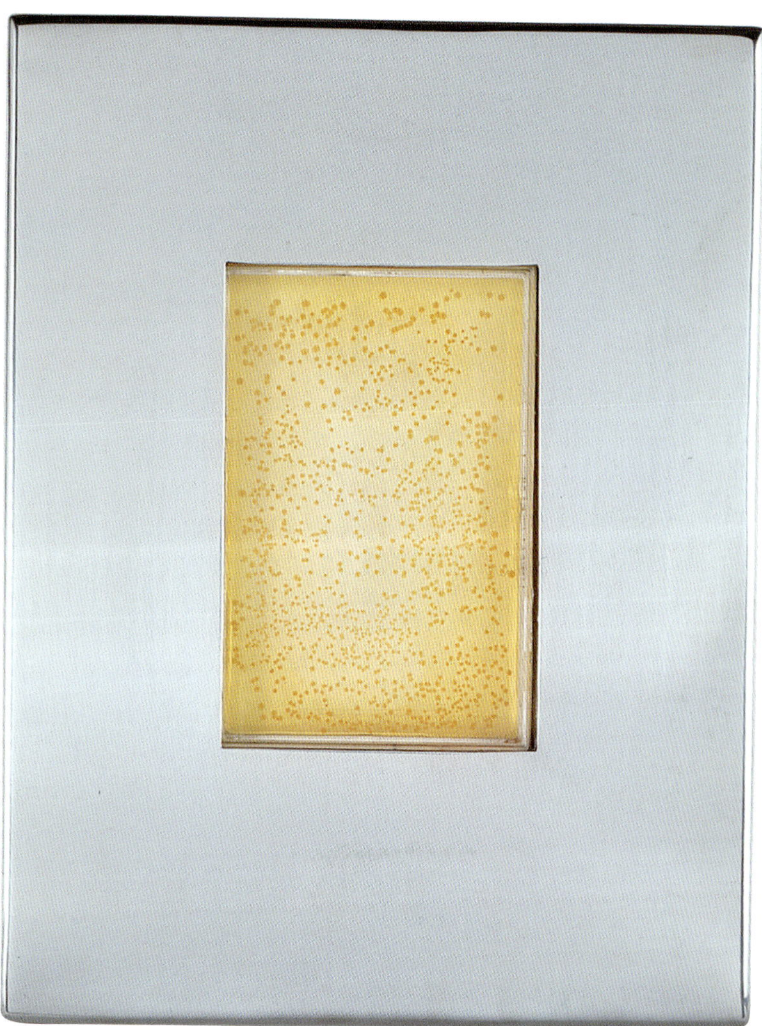

Sir John Sulston
Marc Quinn (b.1964)
Sample of sitter's DNA in agar jelly
mounted in stainless steel, 2001
127 x 85mm (inside frame)
NPG 6591

Marc Quinn's portrait of the Nobel Prize-winning scientist Sir John Sulston (b.1942) took portraiture beyond the assumption that it has to depict a sitter's appearance. Instead, in this work Quinn evokes the presence of the subject directly, intimately and organically. As founding director (1992–2000) of the Sanger Centre, Cambridge, Sulston's work involving DNA cloning led to the decoding of the human genetic sequence. This pivotal achievement enabled a reading of the DNA instructions that define an individual human being. Commissioned by the National Portrait Gallery, Quinn used a process similar to the sitter's methods for DNA cloning. Fragments of Sulston's DNA were treated so that they could be contained in bacteria. Each spot is a colony grown from a single bacterial cell, which was then stabilised. With its source in Sulston's genes, the portrait identifies him uniquely, providing the essential information that is his starting point.

National Trust properties

The National Trust is a charity with a love for preserving historic places and spaces across England, Wales and Northern Ireland. The Trust protects over 350 historic houses and gardens, 1,100km of coastline, 254,000 hectares of countryside and six World Heritage sites – for ever, for everyone.

Many of the sitters featured in this book are associated with National Trust properties.

To find out when properties are open to visit, admission prices, membership and much else besides, please visit www.nationaltrust.org.uk or telephone 0844 800 1895.

The Beatles' Childhood Homes: 20 Forthlin Road and 'Mendips'
Woolton and Allerton, Liverpool
John Lennon and Paul McCartney of The Beatles' childhood homes.

Chartwell
Westerham, Kent TN16 1PS
Family home and garden of Sir Winston Churchill.

Cliveden
Taplow, Maidenhead SL6 0JA
Home to the Astors and where the Profumo affair began. A popular retreat among Royalty, it is now a hotel with incredible gardens.

Clouds Hill
Wareham, Dorset BH20 7NQ
Rural retreat of T.E. Lawrence (Laurence of Arabia) in the heart of Dorset.

Knole
Sevenoaks, Kent TN15 0RP
Childhood home of Vita Sackville-West and inspiration for Virginia Woolf's *Orlando*.

Monk's House
Lewes, East Sussex BN7 3H5
Country retreat of novelist Virginia Woolf.

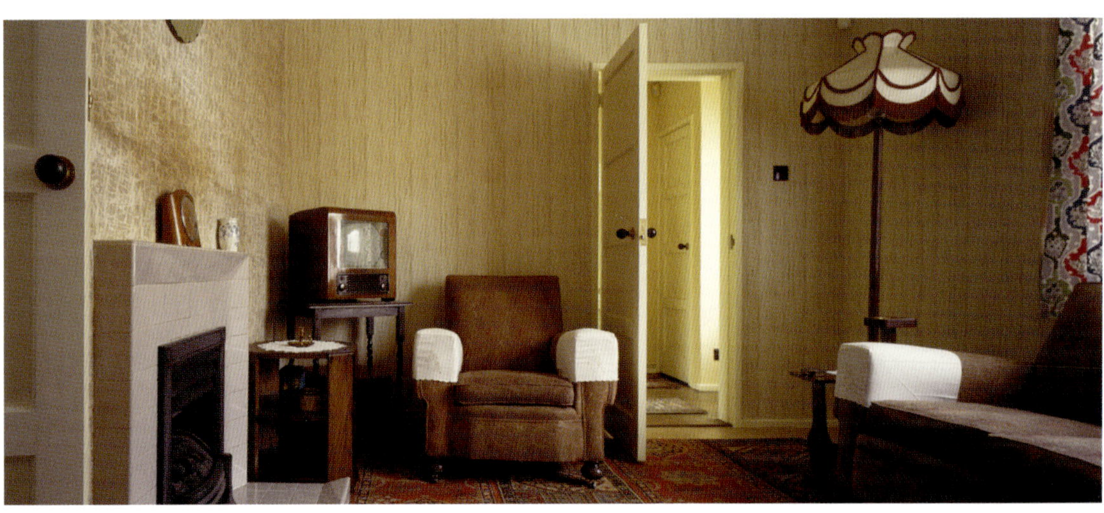
20 Forthlin Road, Liverpool

National Portrait Gallery

Sissinghurst Castle
Cranbrook, Kent TN17 2AB
World-renowned gardens
designed by Vita Sackville-West
and Harold Nicolson.

Stowe
Buckingham MK18 5EQ
Designed by Lord Cobham,
the eighteenth-century grounds
at Stowe are a fine example of
English landscape gardens.

Waddesdon Manor
Buckinghamshire HP18 0JH
Rothschild family estate inherited
and restored by Jacob Rothschild,
4th Baron Rothschild.

Wightwick Manor
Wolverhampton,
West Midlands WV6 8EE
Arts & Crafts-furnished home
filled with a heady collection of
Pre-Raphaelite art and Morris &
Co. furnishings.

2 Willow Road
Hampstead, London NW3 1TH
Modernist home designed by
architect Ernö Goldfinger.
Please check opening times
before visiting.

The National Portrait Gallery
was founded in 1856 'to promote
through the medium of portraits
the appreciation of men and
women who have made and are
making British culture.' Victorian
and Edwardian portraits from its
extensive Collection are displayed
on the first floor. Early twentieth-
century portraits are displayed in
Room 31 (below) on the first floor.
Displayed on glass walls, this
transparent arrangement evokes
a gathering of leading men and
women associated with the period
1919–59, an era that witnessed
radical changes affecting every
aspect of life.

The National Portrait Gallery has
a number of regional partners in
whose properties works from the
Collection are displayed.

Beyond the Gallery
The Gallery is committed to
making the national collection
of British portraits available
around the country through an
active programme of events,
partnerships and loaned works.
Over 1,150 works are on long-term
loan to 173 venues and the Gallery
also lends to exhibitions organised
by other UK venues. In addition,
items from the Collection are
displayed in period country house
contexts: works from the sixteenth
and seventeenth centuries can
be seen at Montacute House
in Somerset (National Trust),
works from the eighteenth
century at Beningbrough Hall in
North Yorkshire (National Trust),
and works from the nineteenth
century at Bodelwyddan Castle in
Denbighshire.

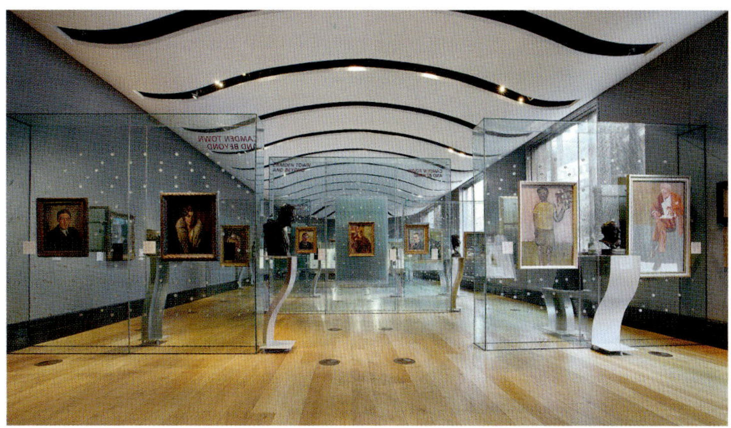

Room 31, National Portrait Gallery, London

Index of artists and sitters